Curtiss Hill

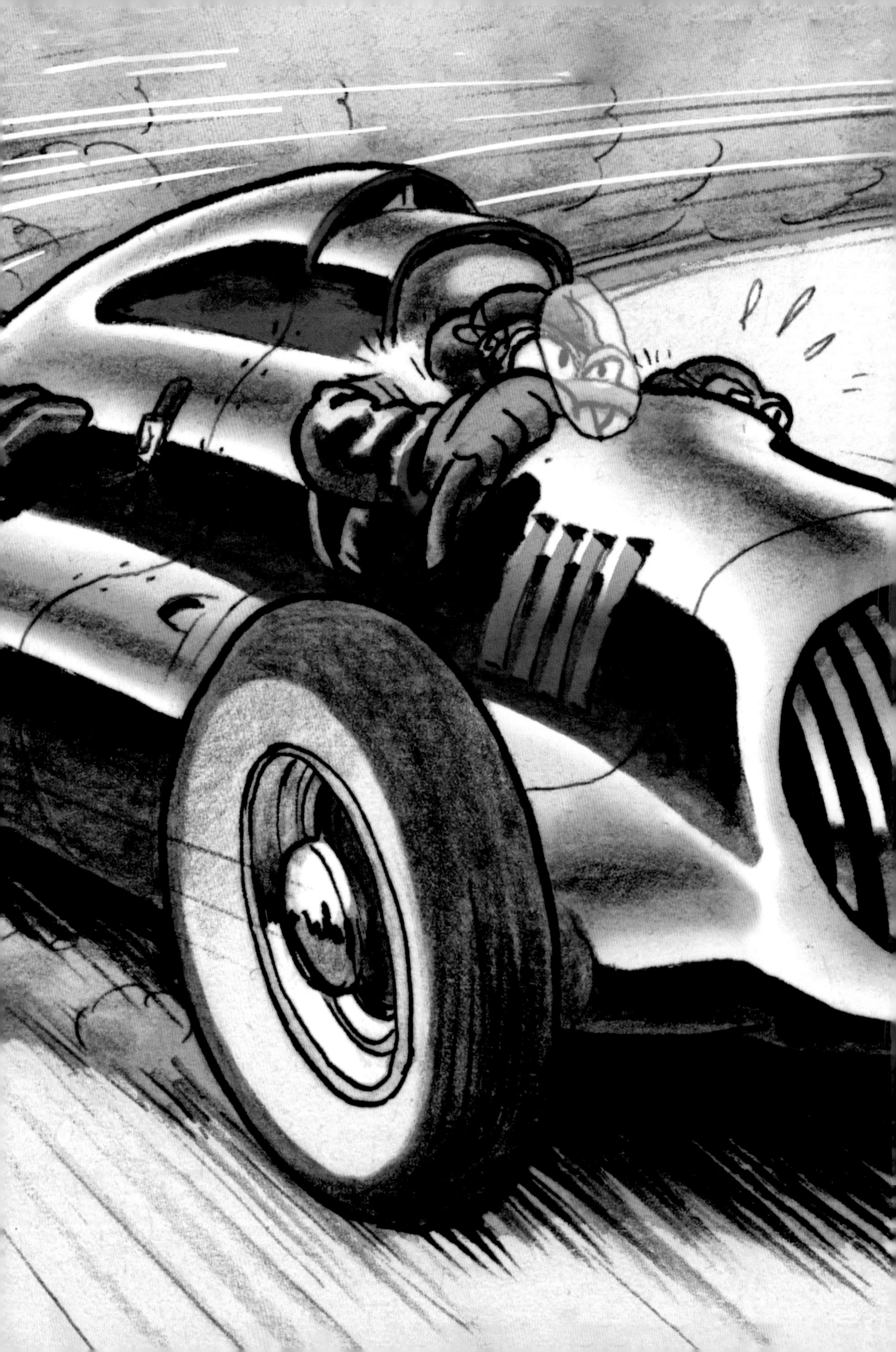

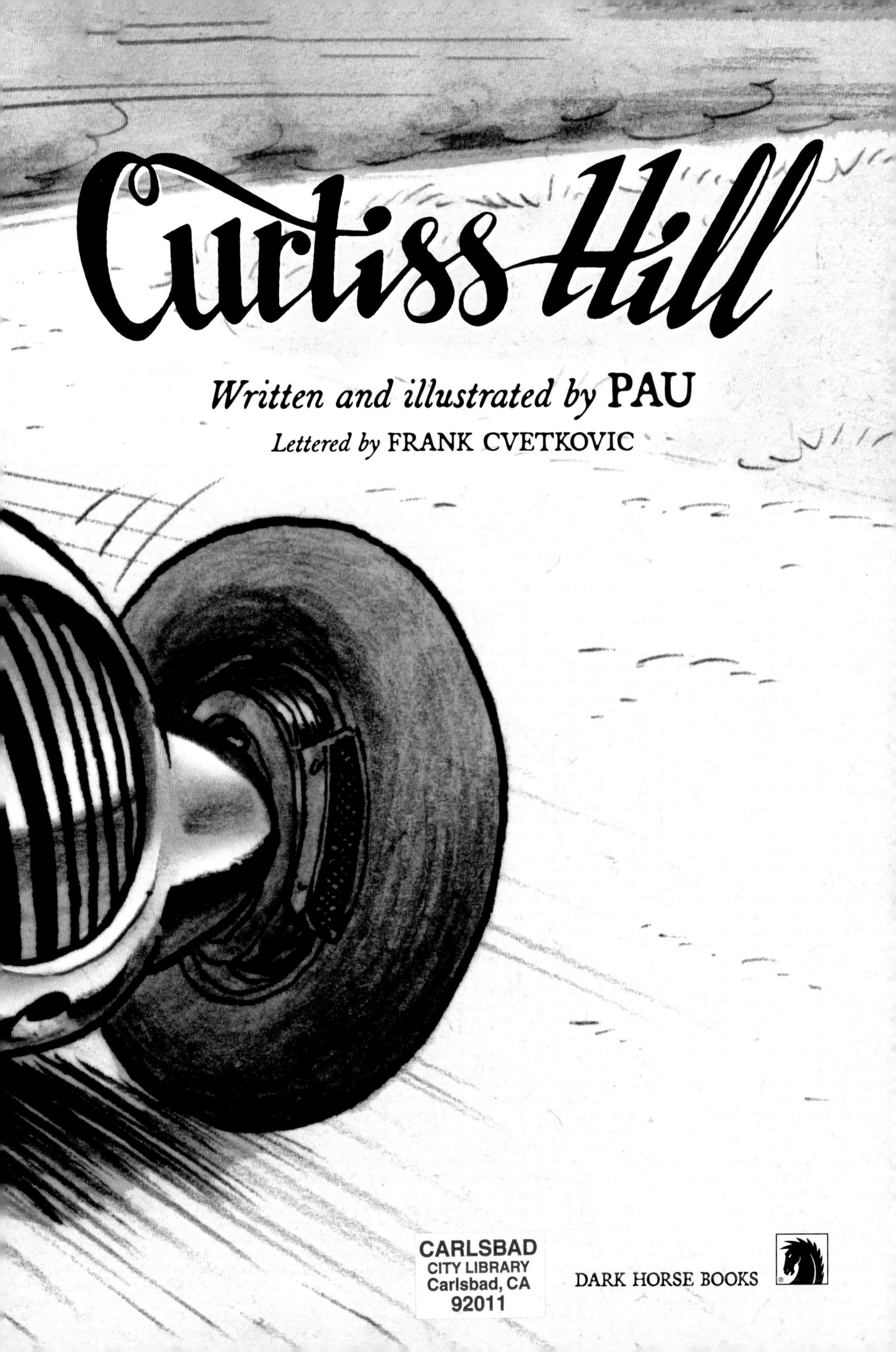

Curtiss Hill

Written and illustrated by **PAU**

Lettered by FRANK CVETKOVIC

DARK HORSE BOOKS

President and Publisher MIKE RICHARDSON

Editor MEGAN WALKER

Assistant Editor JUDY KHUU

Designer PATRICK SATTERFIELD

Digital Art Technician ANN GRAY

Published by Dark Horse Books
A division of Dark Horse Comics LLC
10956 SE Main Street • Milwaukie, OR 97222

DarkHorse.com

 Facebook.com/DarkHorseComics
 Twitter.com/DarkHorseComics

To find a comics shop in your area, visit comicshoplocator.com

First Edition: March 2021
Ebook ISBN 978-1-50672-515-4
Trade Paperback ISBN 978-1-50672-360-0

1 3 5 7 9 10 8 6 4 2
Printed in China

Library of Congress Cataloging-in-Publication Data

Names: Pau, 1972- writer, illustrator.
Title: Curtiss Hill / written and illustrated by Pau.
Other titles: Curtiss Hill. English
Description: Milwaukie, OR : Dark Horse Books, 2021. | Summary: "A renowned
  racecar driver searches for victory beyond the finish line as he
  uncovers the truth surrounding the sudden disappearance of his
  co-pilot"-- Provided by publisher.
Identifiers: LCCN 2020030319 | ISBN 9781506723600 (paperback)
Subjects: LCSH: Graphic novels.
Classification: LCC PN6777.P38 C8713 2021 | DDC 741.5/946--dc23
LC record available at https://lccn.loc.gov/2020030319

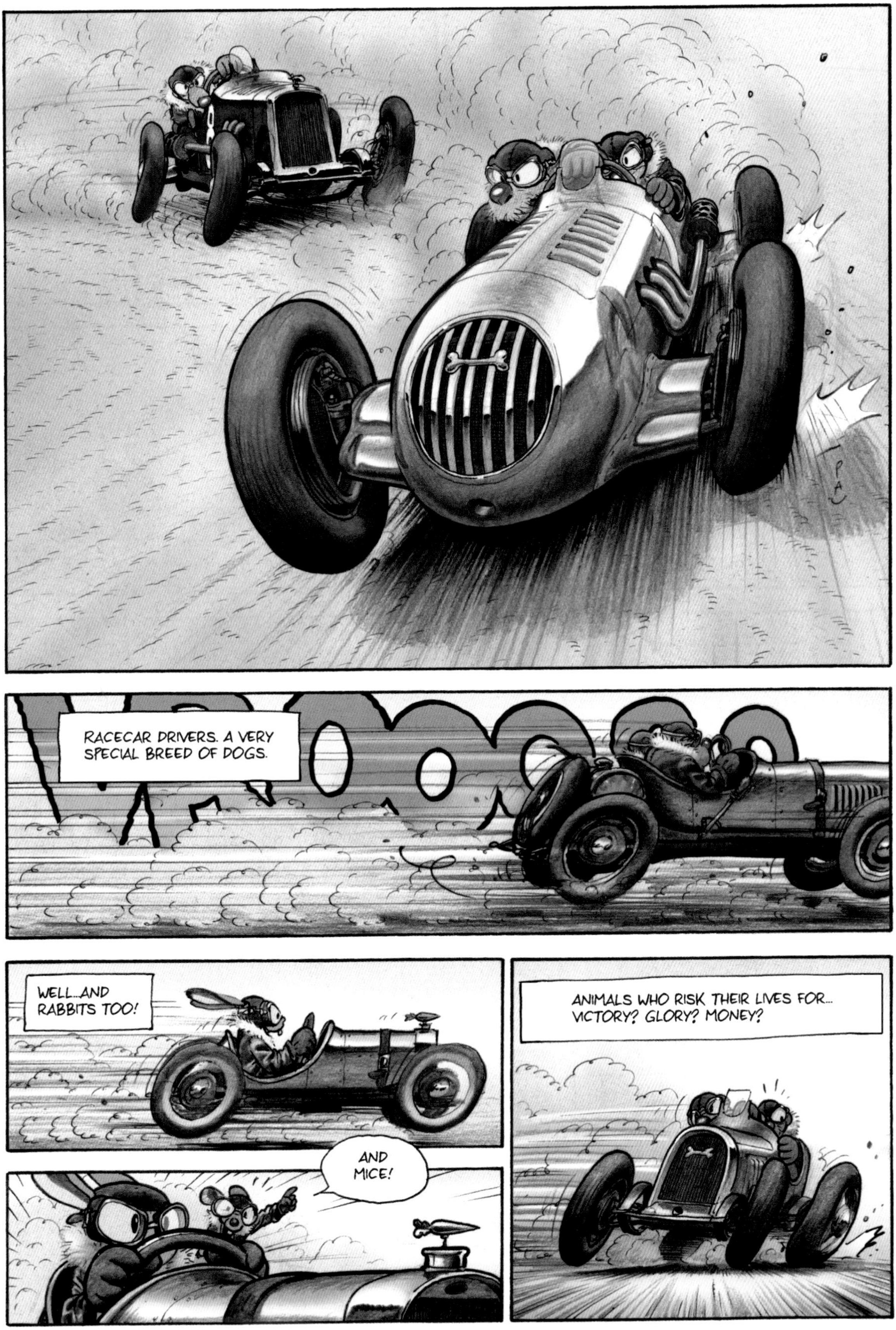
RACECAR DRIVERS. A VERY SPECIAL BREED OF DOGS.
WELL...AND RABBITS TOO!
AND MICE!
ANIMALS WHO RISK THEIR LIVES FOR... VICTORY? GLORY? MONEY?

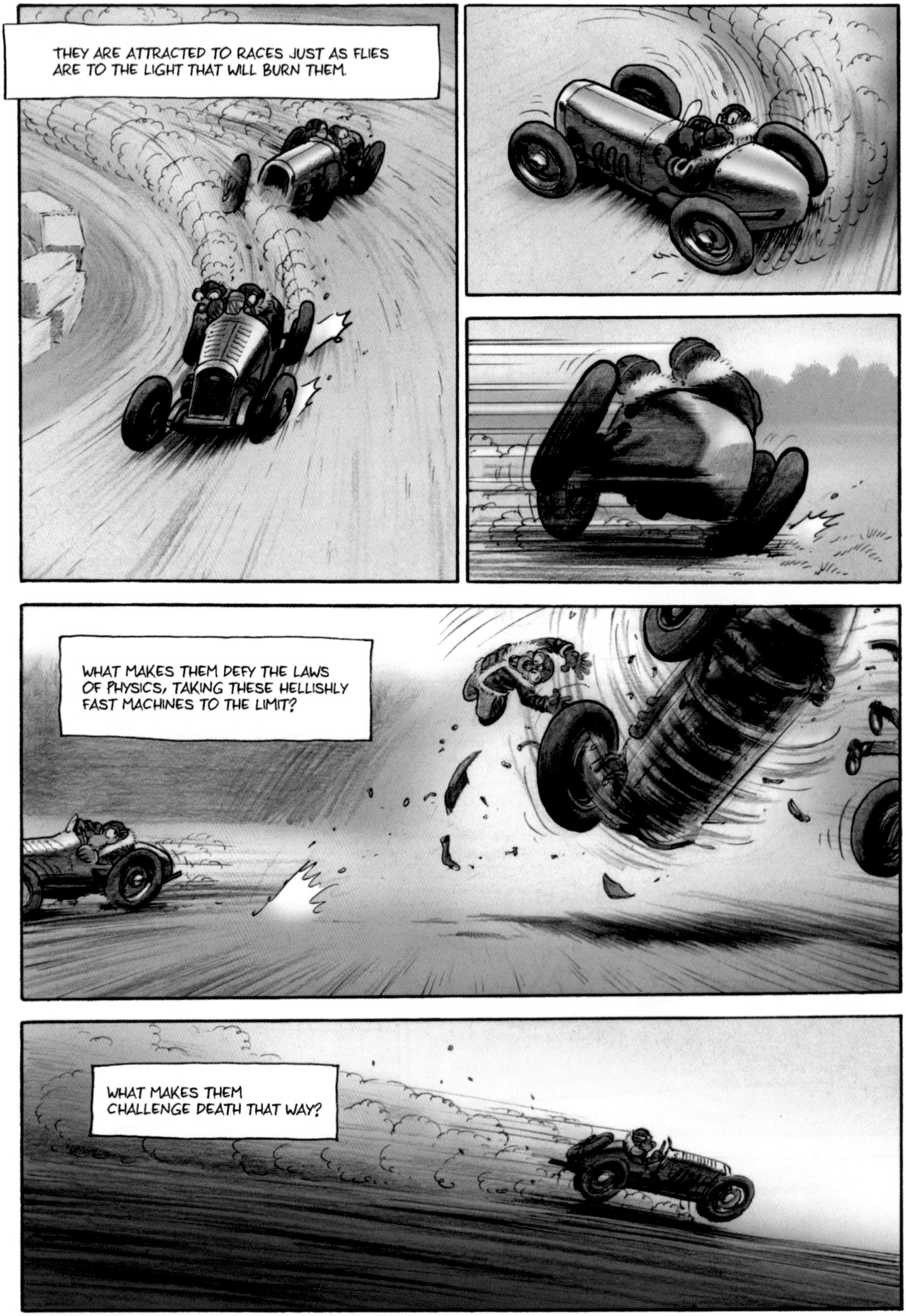
THEY ARE ATTRACTED TO RACES JUST AS FLIES ARE TO THE LIGHT THAT WILL BURN THEM.
WHAT MAKES THEM DEFY THE LAWS OF PHYSICS, TAKING THESE HELLISHLY FAST MACHINES TO THE LIMIT?
WHAT MAKES THEM CHALLENGE DEATH THAT WAY?

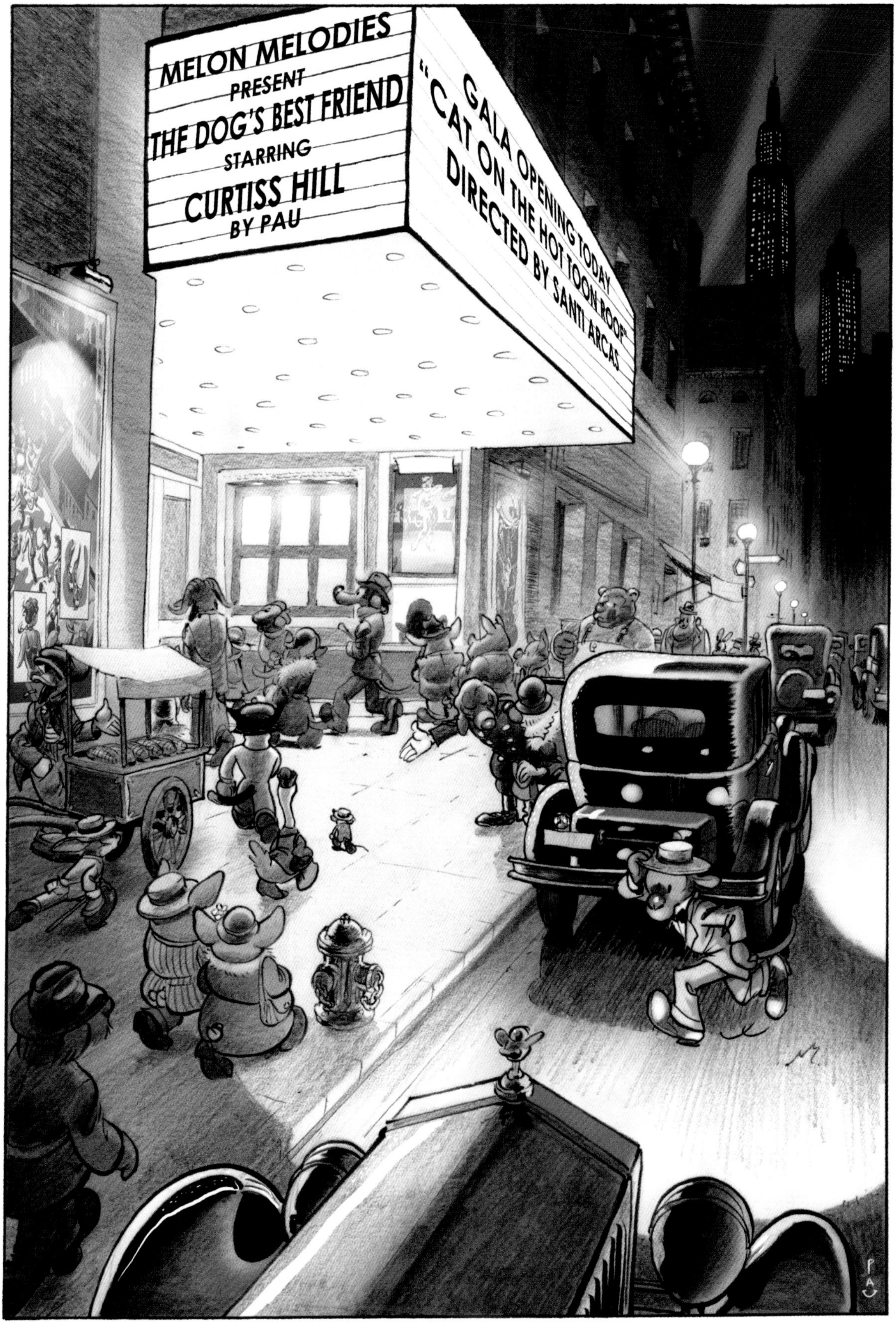
MELON MELODIES
PRESENT
THE DOG'S BEST FRIEND
STARRING
CURTISS HILL
BY PAU
GALA OPENING TODAY
"CAT ON THE HOT TOON ROOF"
DIRECTED BY SANTI ARCAS
PAU

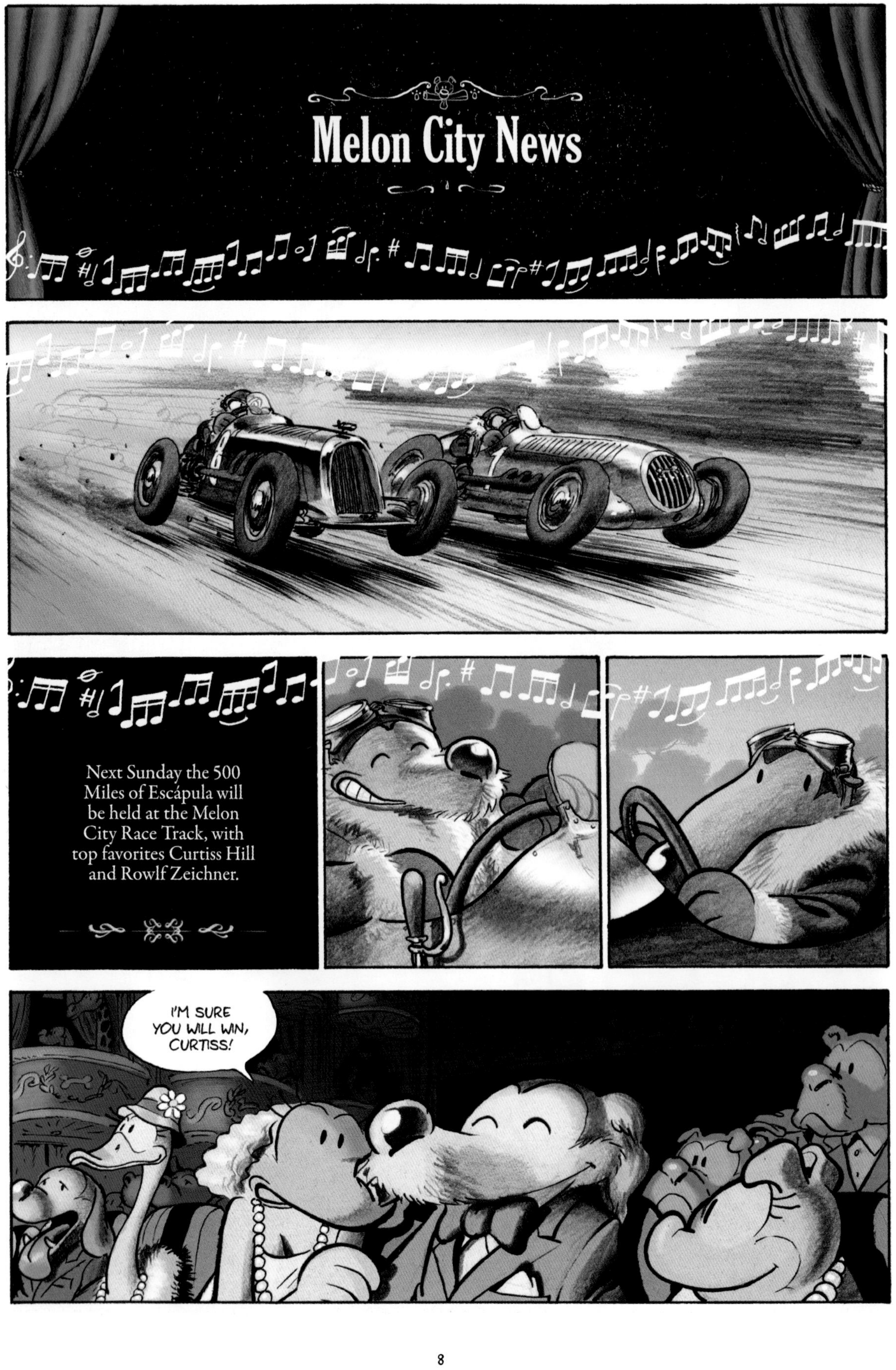
Melon City News
Next Sunday the 500 Miles of Escápula will be held at the Melon City Race Track, with top favorites Curtiss Hill and Rowlf Zeichner.
I'M SURE YOU WILL WIN, CURTISS!

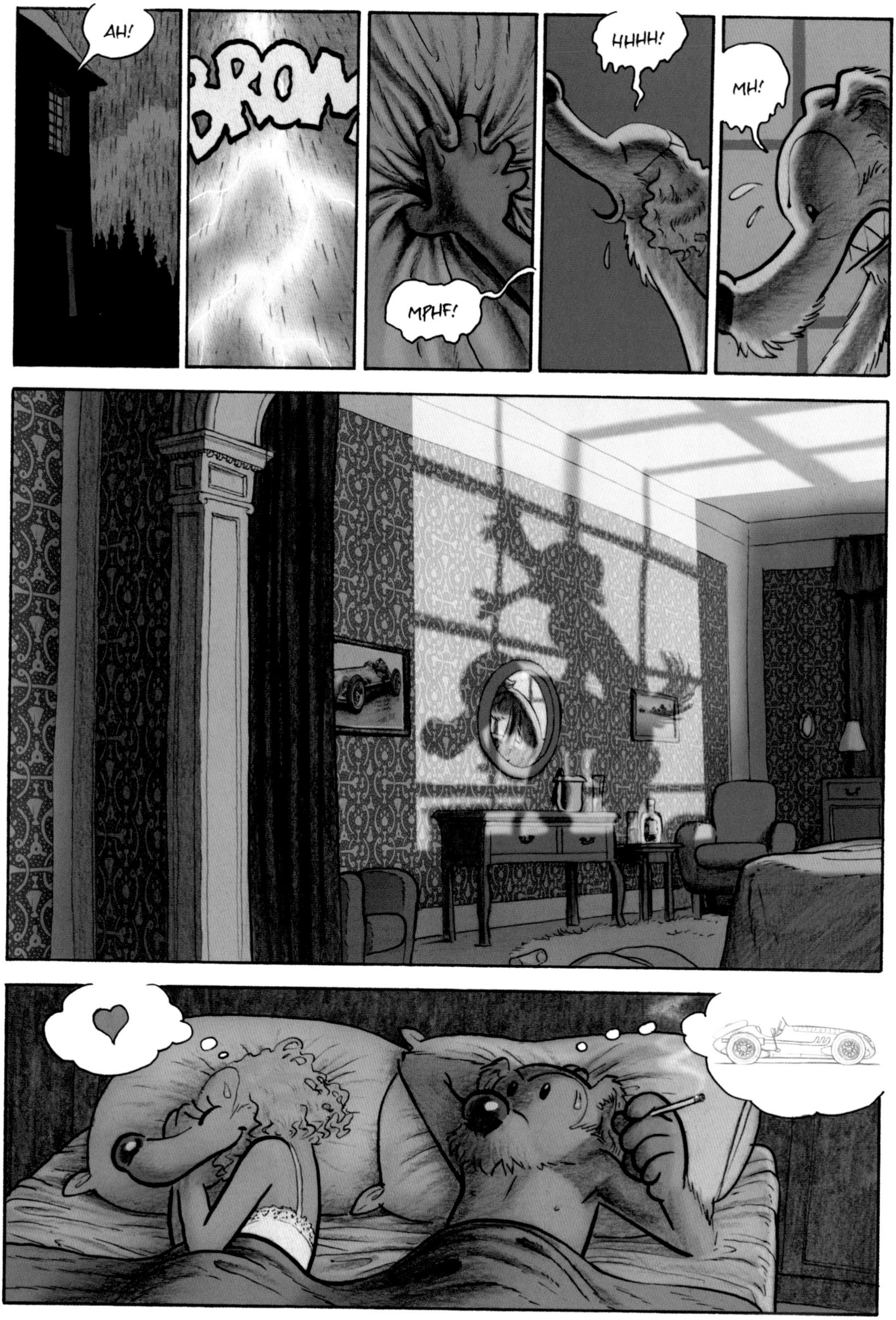
AH!
MPHF!
HHHH!
MH!

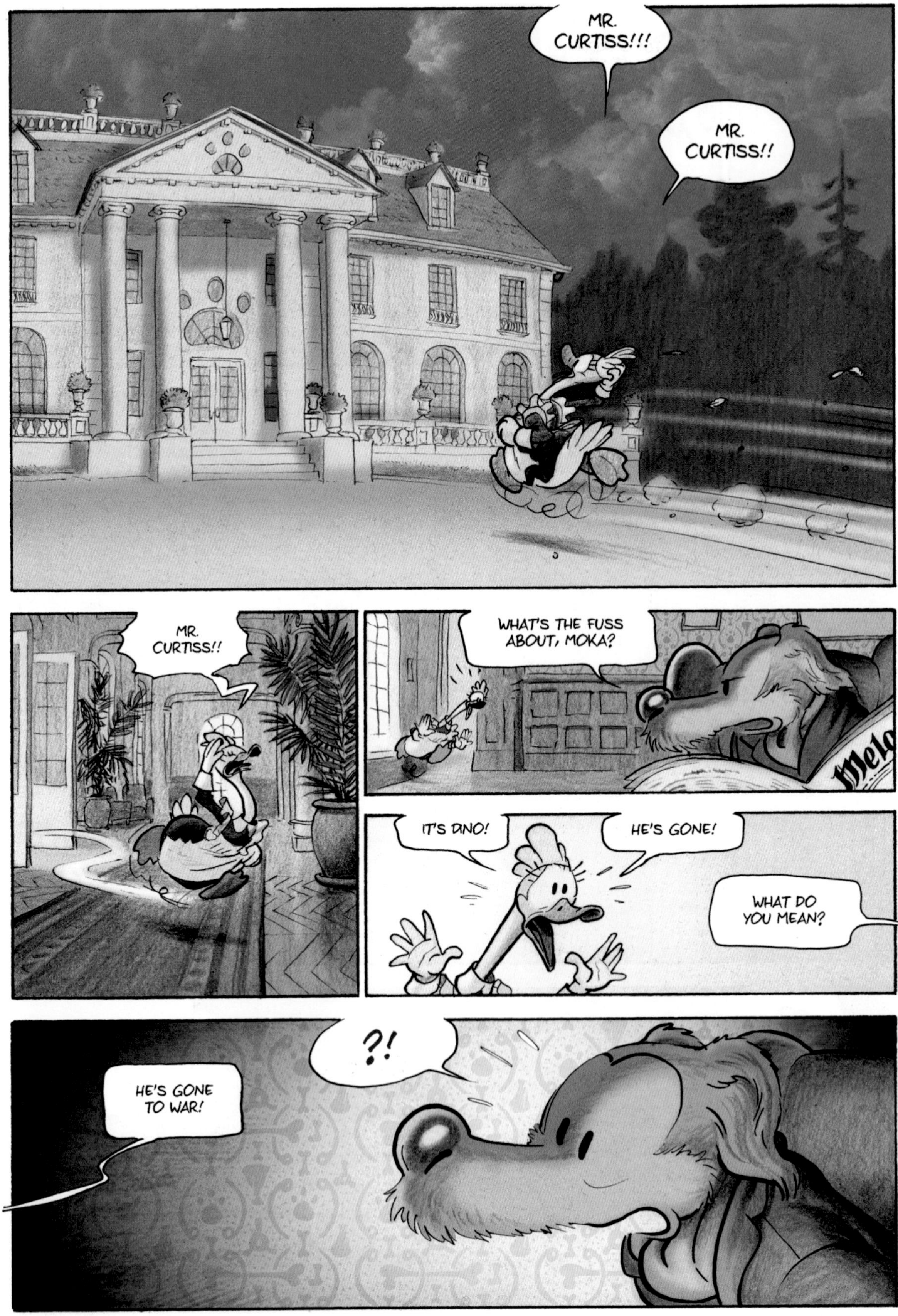

MR. CURTISS!!!
MR. CURTISS!!
MR. CURTISS!!
WHAT'S THE FUSS ABOUT, MOKA?
IT'S DINO!
HE'S GONE!
WHAT DO YOU MEAN?
?!
HE'S GONE TO WAR!

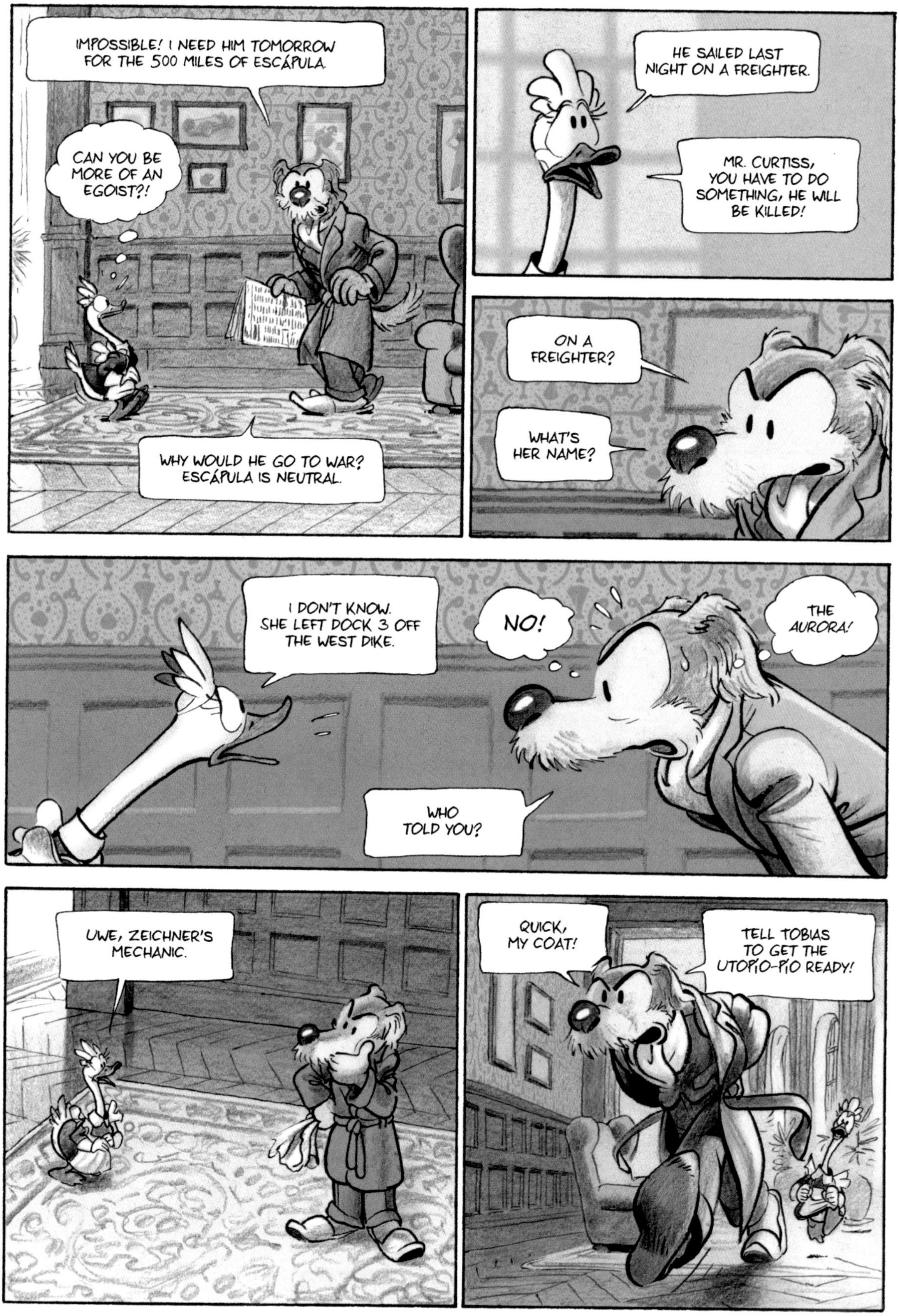

IMPOSSIBLE! I NEED HIM TOMORROW FOR THE 500 MILES OF ESCÁPULA.
CAN YOU BE MORE OF AN EGOIST?!
WHY WOULD HE GO TO WAR? ESCÁPULA IS NEUTRAL.
HE SAILED LAST NIGHT ON A FREIGHTER.
MR. CURTISS, YOU HAVE TO DO SOMETHING, HE WILL BE KILLED!
ON A FREIGHTER?
WHAT'S HER NAME?
I DON'T KNOW. SHE LEFT DOCK 3 OFF THE WEST DIKE.
NO!
THE AURORA!
WHO TOLD YOU?
UWE, ZEICHNER'S MECHANIC.
QUICK, MY COAT!
TELL TOBIAS TO GET THE UTOPÍO-PÍO READY!

WHY?

MR. CURTISS,
THE CAR IS READY.

VROMVROMVROMVROMVROM

CLAP

FRROOAAR

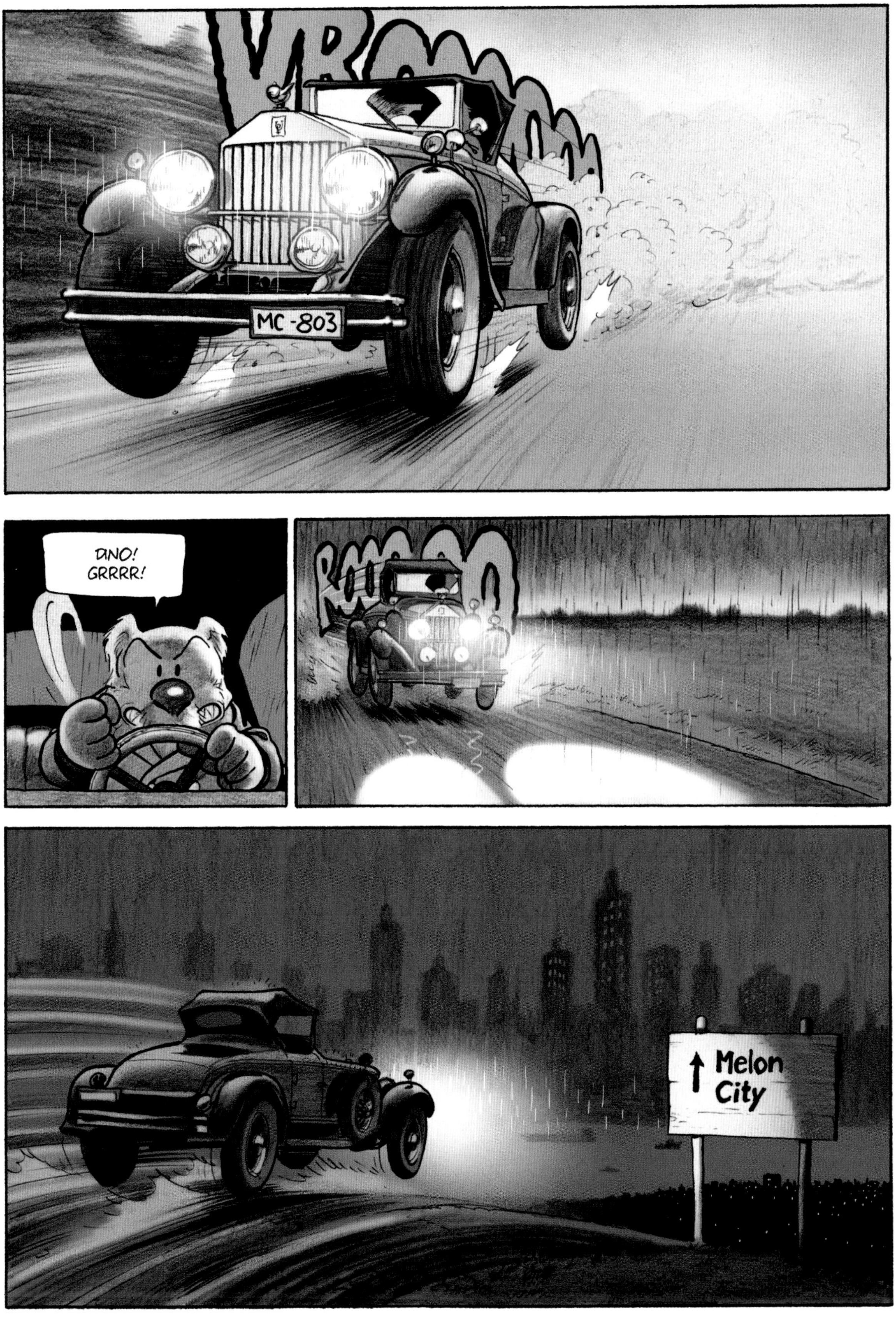
MC-803
DINO!
GRRRR!
↑ Melon
City

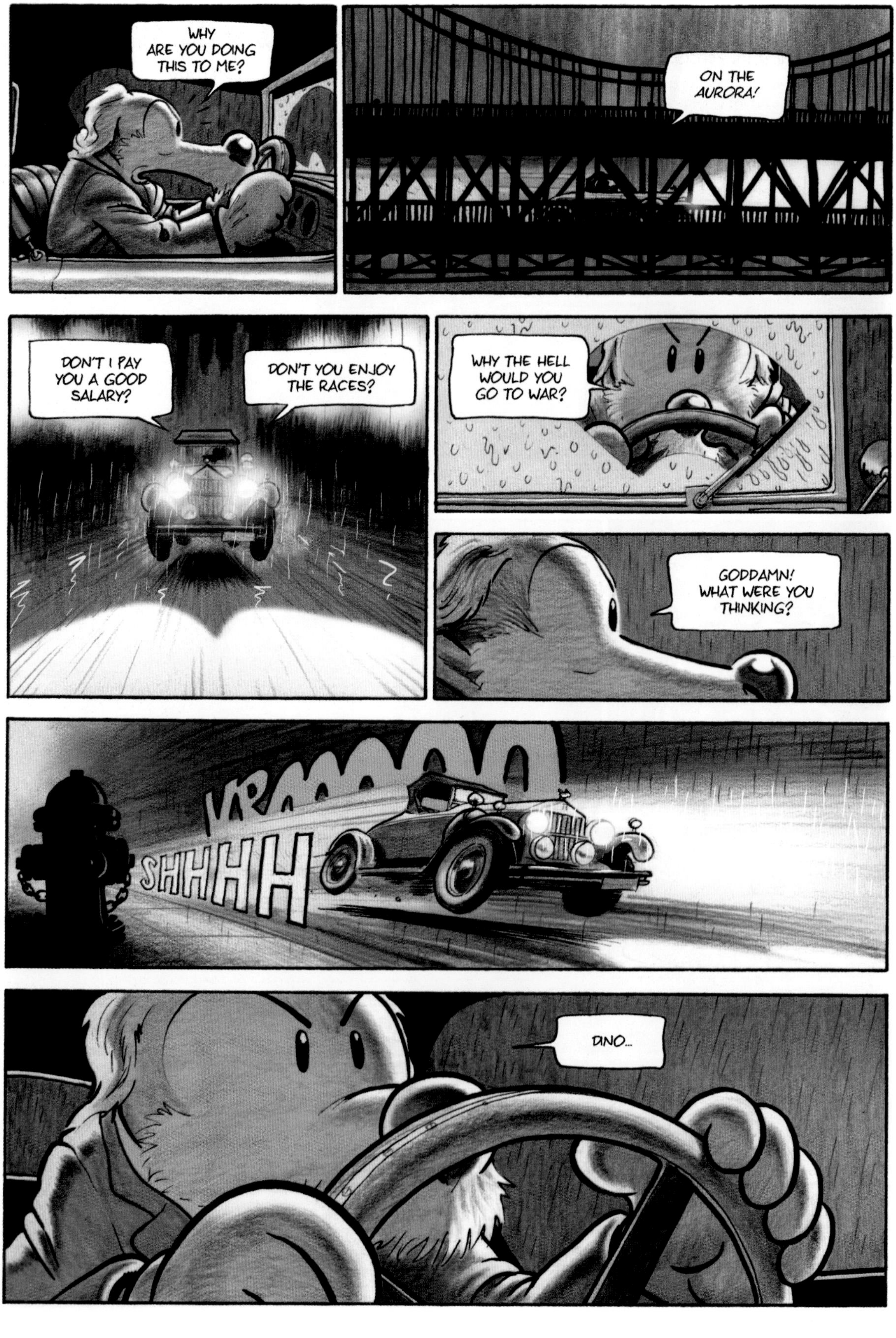
WHY ARE YOU DOING THIS TO ME?
ON THE AURORA!
DON'T I PAY YOU A GOOD SALARY?
DON'T YOU ENJOY THE RACES?
WHY THE HELL WOULD YOU GO TO WAR?
GODDAMN! WHAT WERE YOU THINKING?
VRMMMM
SHHHH
DINO...

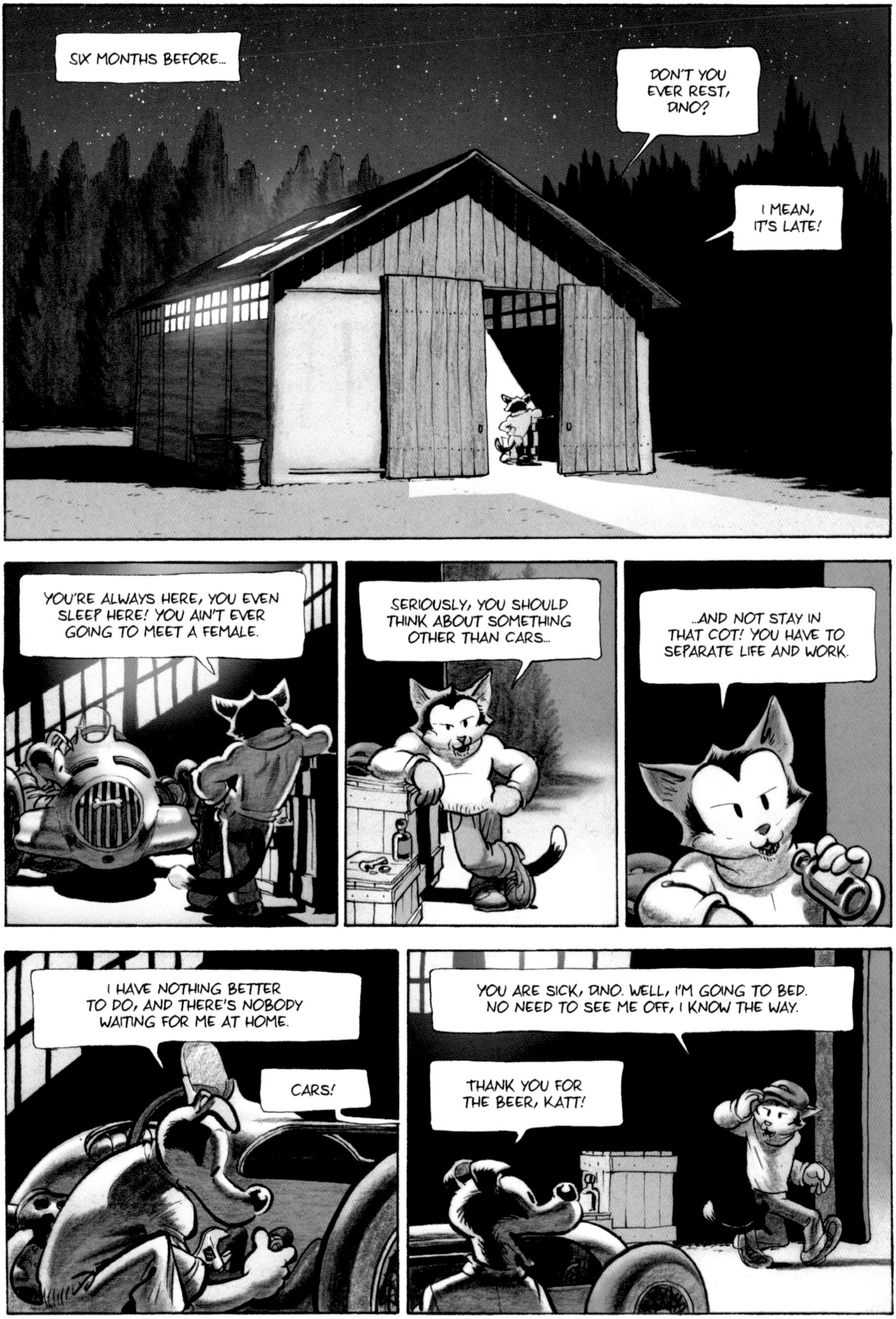
SIX MONTHS BEFORE...
DON'T YOU EVER REST, DINO?
I MEAN, IT'S LATE!
YOU'RE ALWAYS HERE, YOU EVEN SLEEP HERE! YOU AIN'T EVER GOING TO MEET A FEMALE.
SERIOUSLY, YOU SHOULD THINK ABOUT SOMETHING OTHER THAN CARS...
...AND NOT STAY IN THAT COT! YOU HAVE TO SEPARATE LIFE AND WORK.
I HAVE NOTHING BETTER TO DO, AND THERE'S NOBODY WAITING FOR ME AT HOME.
CARS!
YOU ARE SICK, DINO. WELL, I'M GOING TO BED. NO NEED TO SEE ME OFF, I KNOW THE WAY.
THANK YOU FOR THE BEER, KATT!

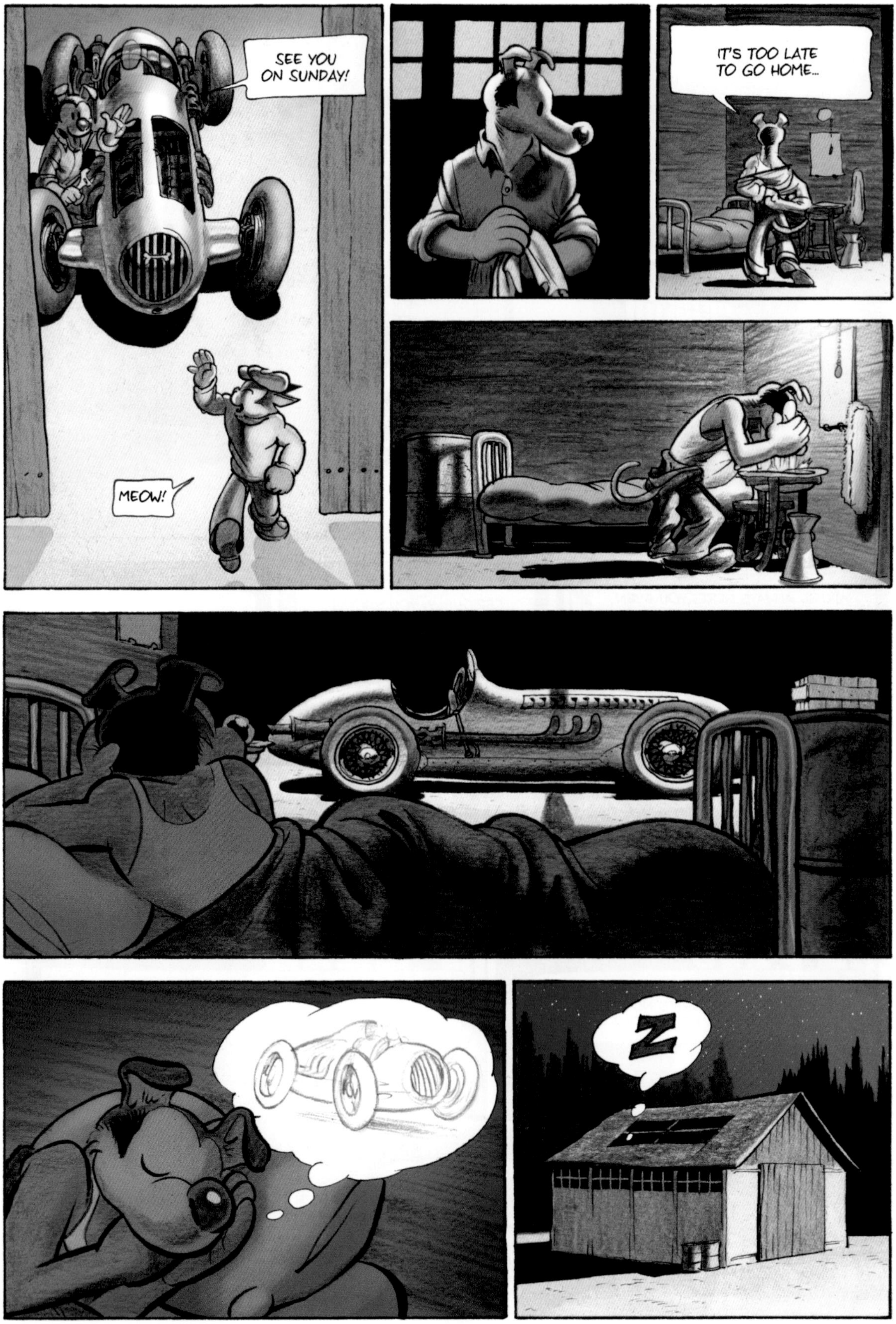
SEE YOU ON SUNDAY!
MEOW!
IT'S TOO LATE TO GO HOME...
Z

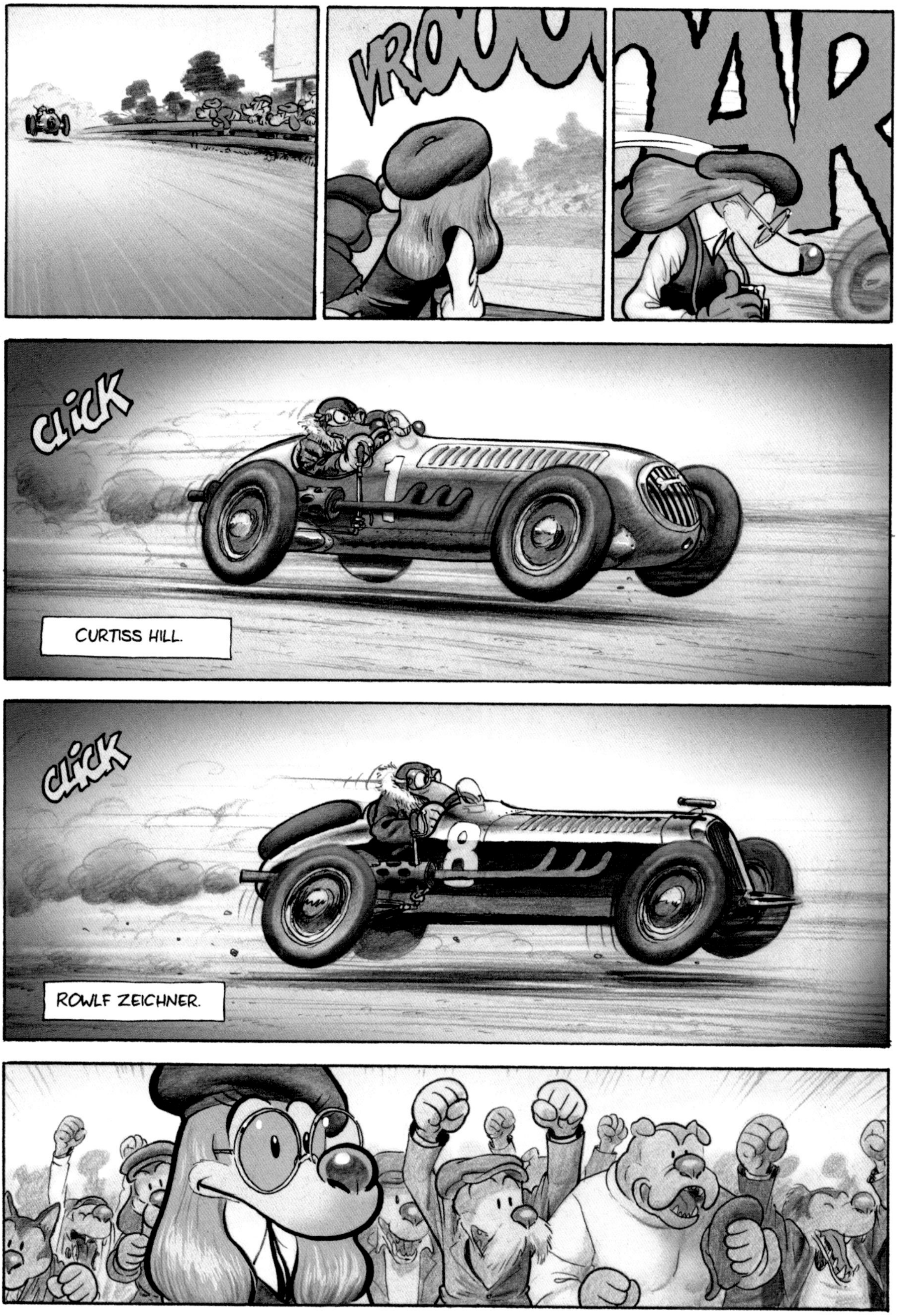
VROOOOAR
CLICK
CURTISS HILL.
CLICK
ROWLF ZEICHNER.

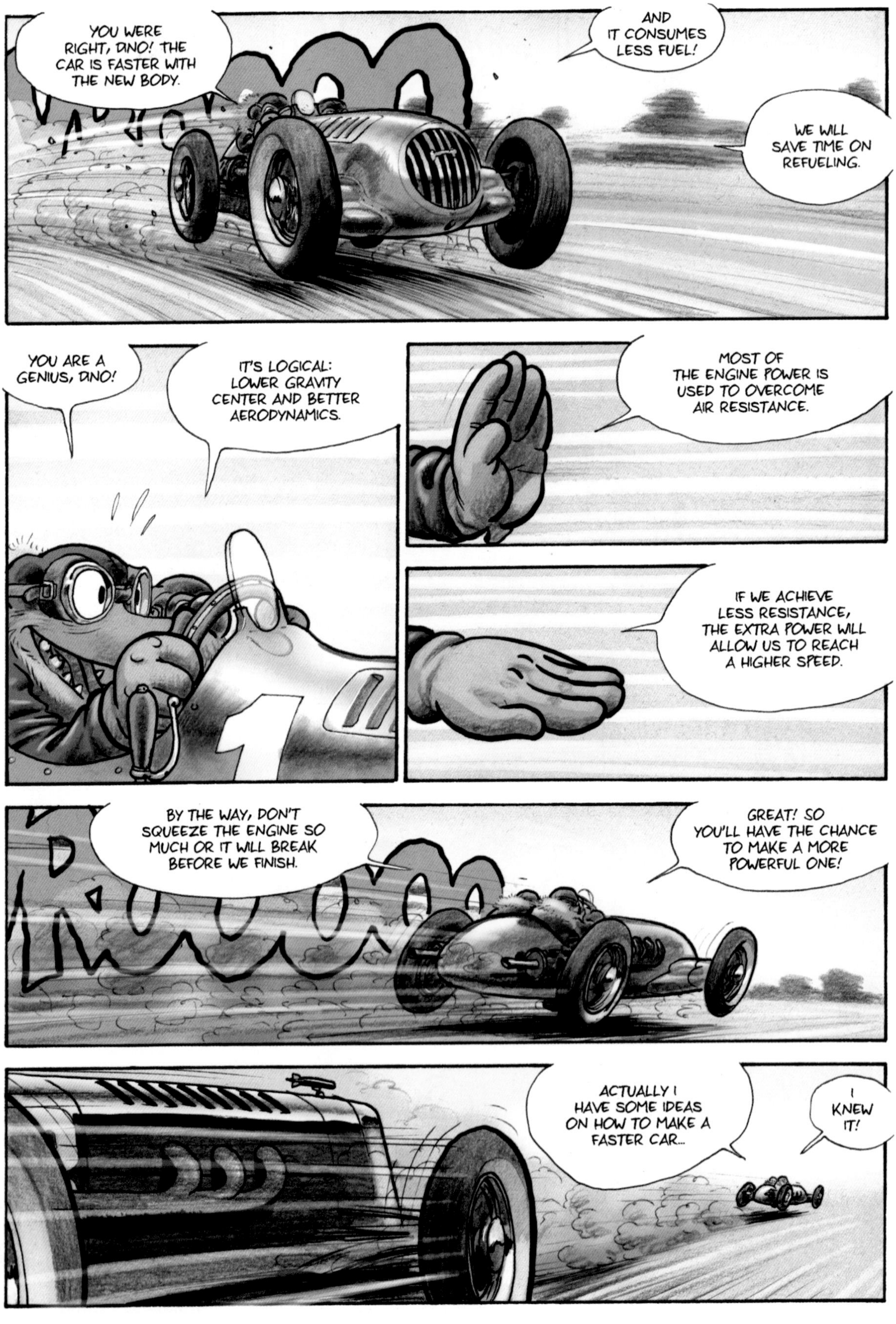
YOU WERE RIGHT, DINO! THE CAR IS FASTER WITH THE NEW BODY.
AND IT CONSUMES LESS FUEL!
WE WILL SAVE TIME ON REFUELING.
YOU ARE A GENIUS, DINO!
IT'S LOGICAL: LOWER GRAVITY CENTER AND BETTER AERODYNAMICS.
MOST OF THE ENGINE POWER IS USED TO OVERCOME AIR RESISTANCE.
IF WE ACHIEVE LESS RESISTANCE, THE EXTRA POWER WILL ALLOW US TO REACH A HIGHER SPEED.
BY THE WAY, DON'T SQUEEZE THE ENGINE SO MUCH OR IT WILL BREAK BEFORE WE FINISH.
GREAT! SO YOU'LL HAVE THE CHANCE TO MAKE A MORE POWERFUL ONE!
ACTUALLY I HAVE SOME IDEAS ON HOW TO MAKE A FASTER CAR...
I KNEW IT!

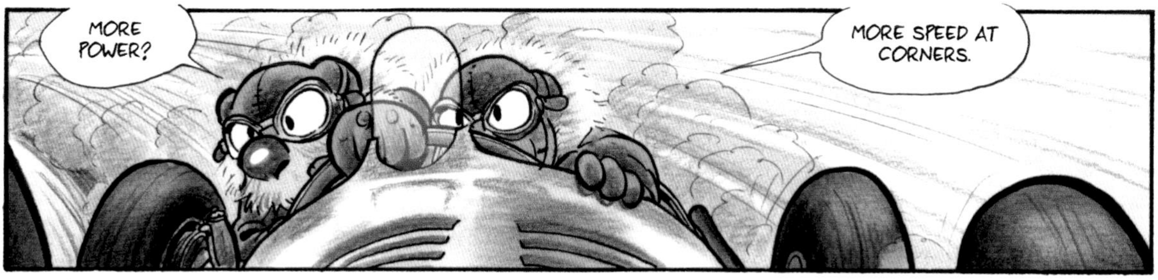
MORE POWER?
MORE SPEED AT CORNERS.

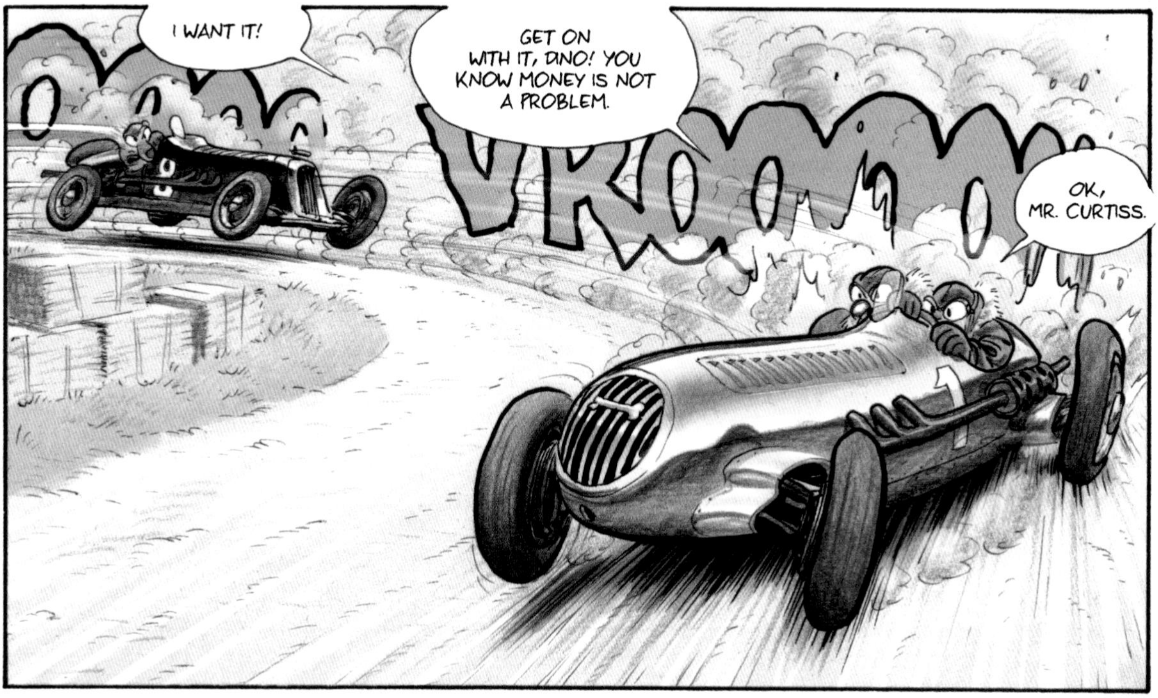
I WANT IT!
GET ON WITH IT, DINO! YOU KNOW MONEY IS NOT A PROBLEM.
VROOMM
OK, MR. CURTISS.

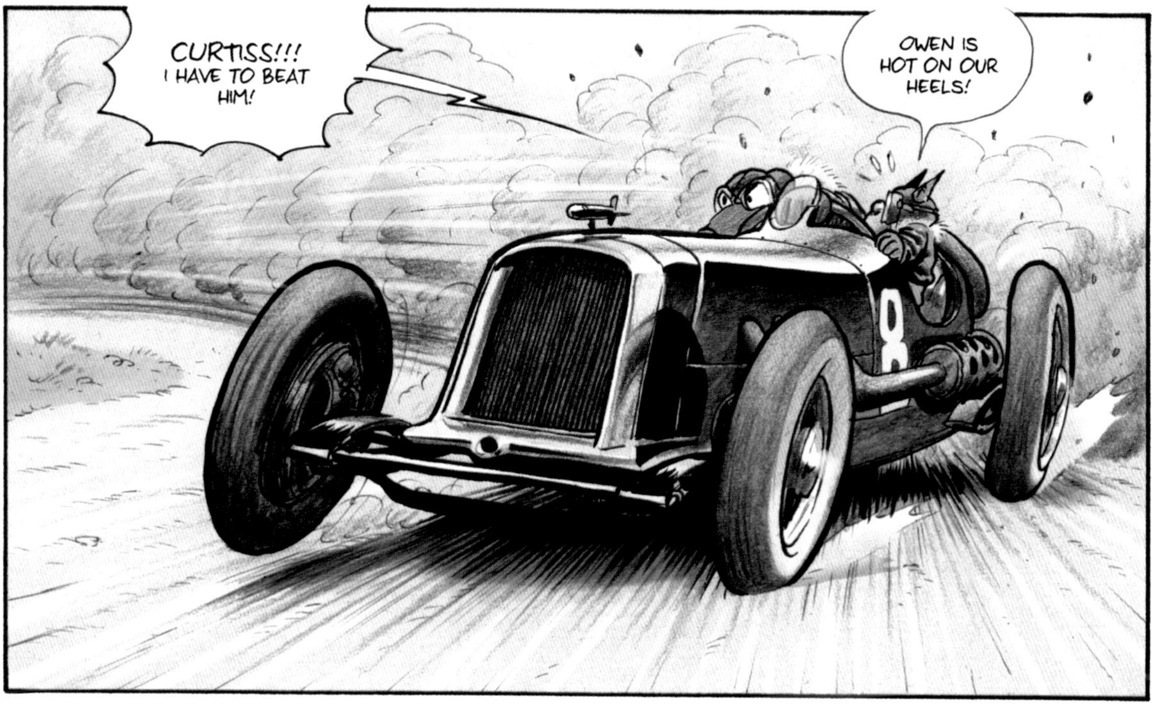
CURTISS!!! I HAVE TO BEAT HIM!
OWEN IS HOT ON OUR HEELS!

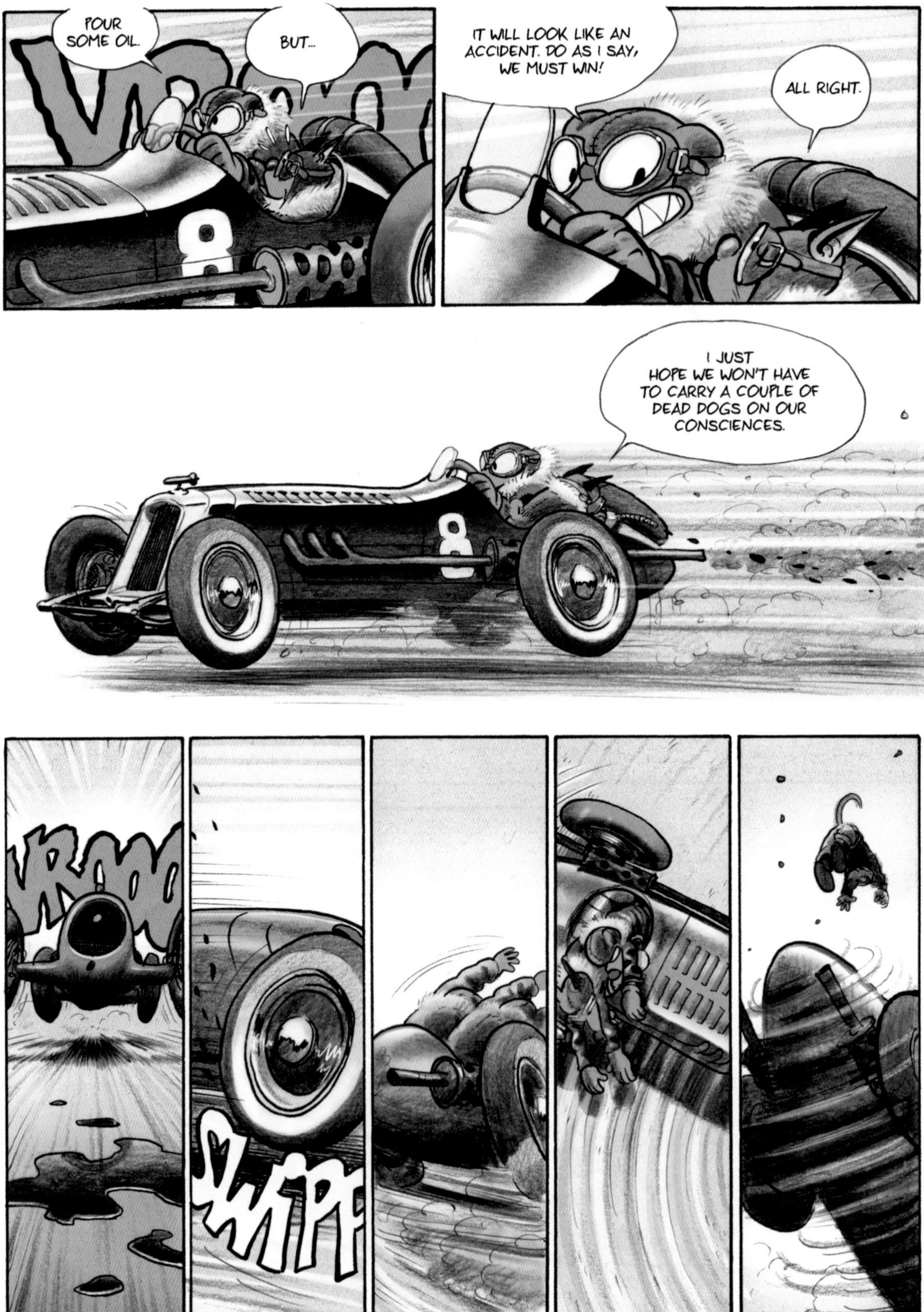

VROOM
POUR SOME OIL.
BUT...
IT WILL LOOK LIKE AN ACCIDENT. DO AS I SAY, WE MUST WIN!
ALL RIGHT.
I JUST HOPE WE WON'T HAVE TO CARRY A COUPLE OF DEAD DOGS ON OUR CONSCIENCES.
VROOO
SWIPP

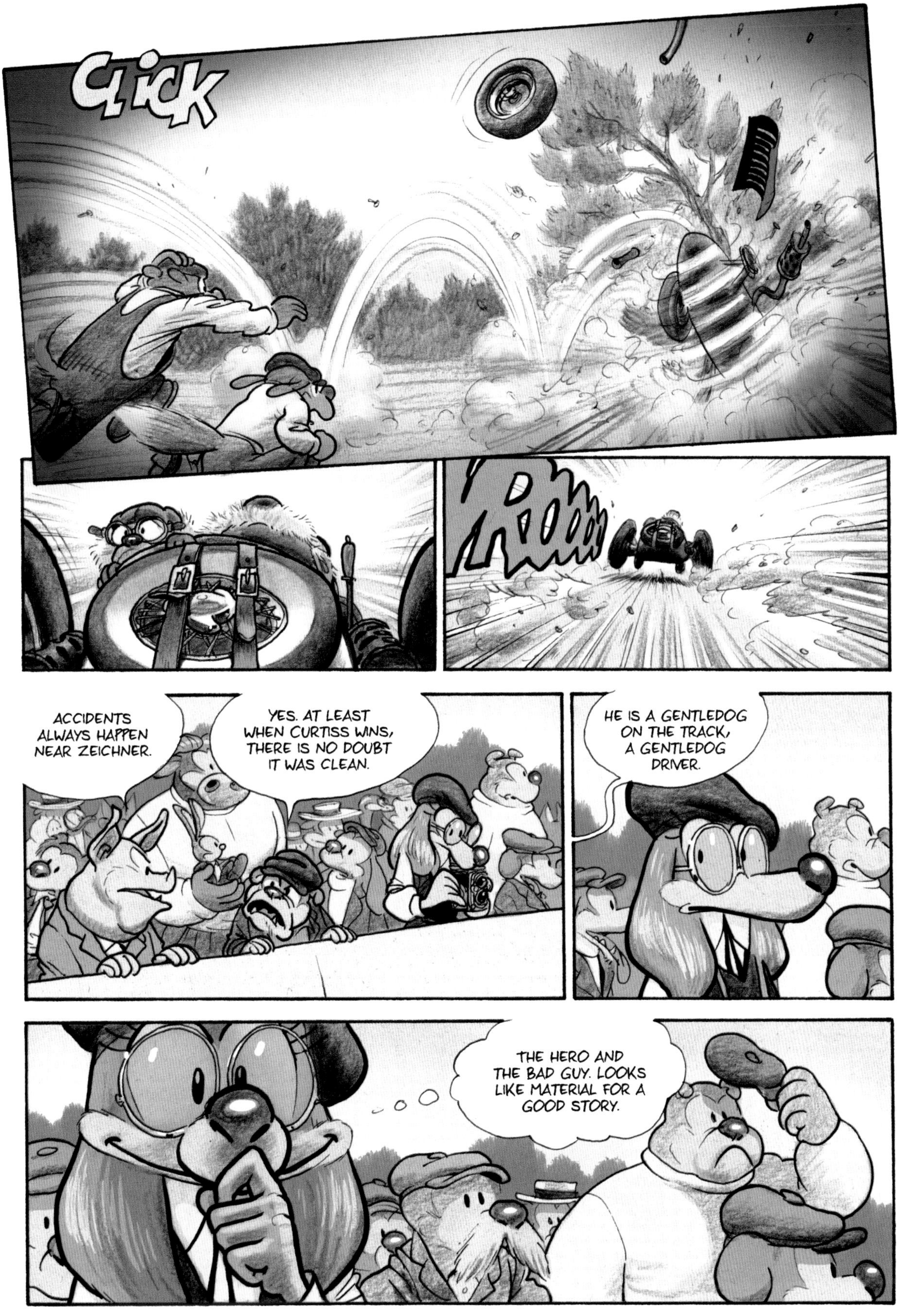
CLICK
RIIIIIII
ACCIDENTS ALWAYS HAPPEN NEAR ZEICHNER.
YES. AT LEAST WHEN CURTISS WINS, THERE IS NO DOUBT IT WAS CLEAN.
HE IS A GENTLEDOG ON THE TRACK, A GENTLEDOG DRIVER.
THE HERO AND THE BAD GUY. LOOKS LIKE MATERIAL FOR A GOOD STORY.

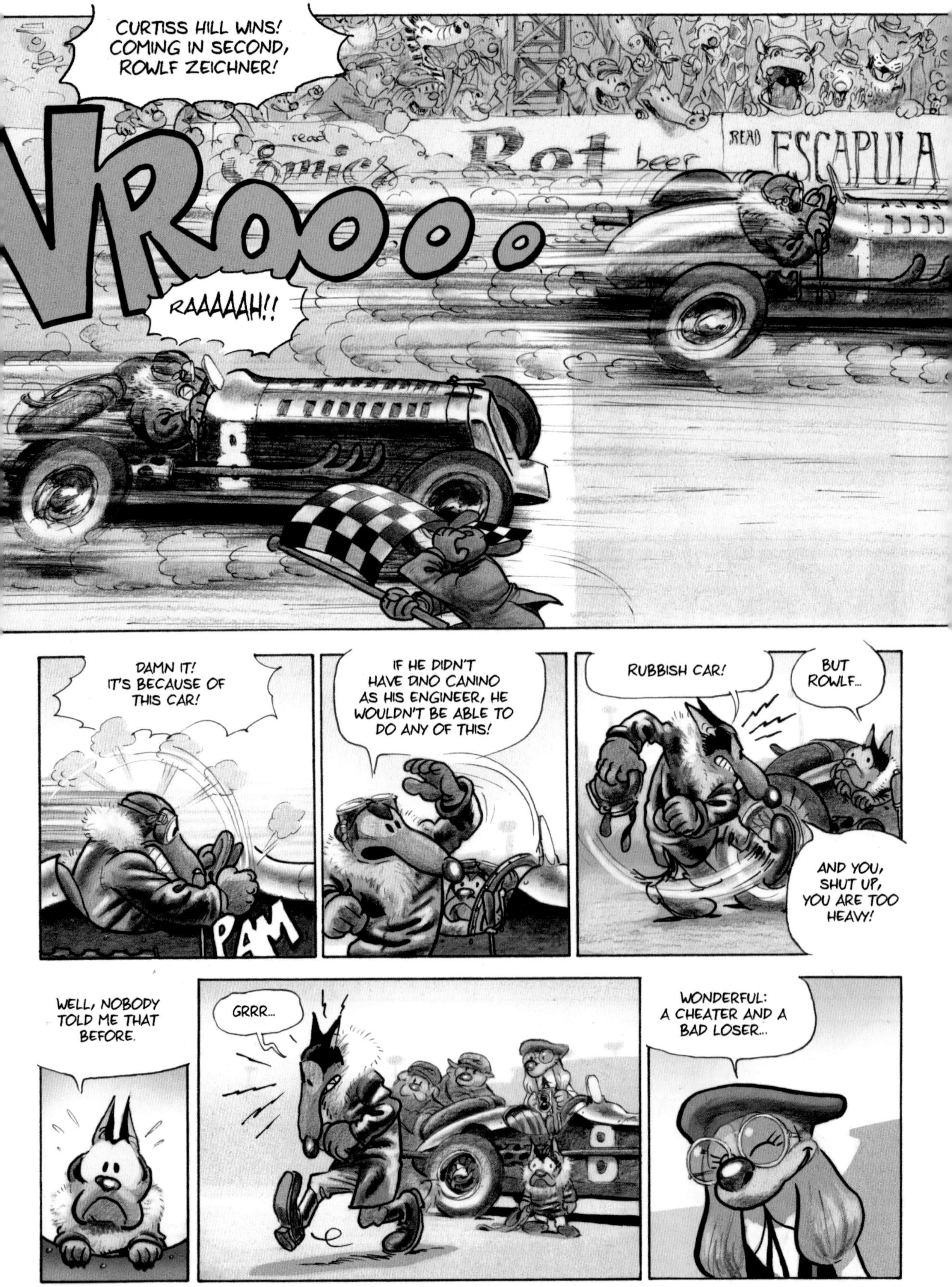
CURTISS HILL WINS! COMING IN SECOND, ROWLF ZEICHNER!
VROOOO...
RAAAAAH!!
read Comics
Rot beer
READ ESCAPULA
DAMN IT! IT'S BECAUSE OF THIS CAR!
PAM
IF HE DIDN'T HAVE DINO CANINO AS HIS ENGINEER, HE WOULDN'T BE ABLE TO DO ANY OF THIS!
RUBBISH CAR!
BUT ROWLF...
AND YOU, SHUT UP, YOU ARE TOO HEAVY!
WELL, NOBODY TOLD ME THAT BEFORE.
GRRR...
WONDERFUL: A CHEATER AND A BAD LOSER...

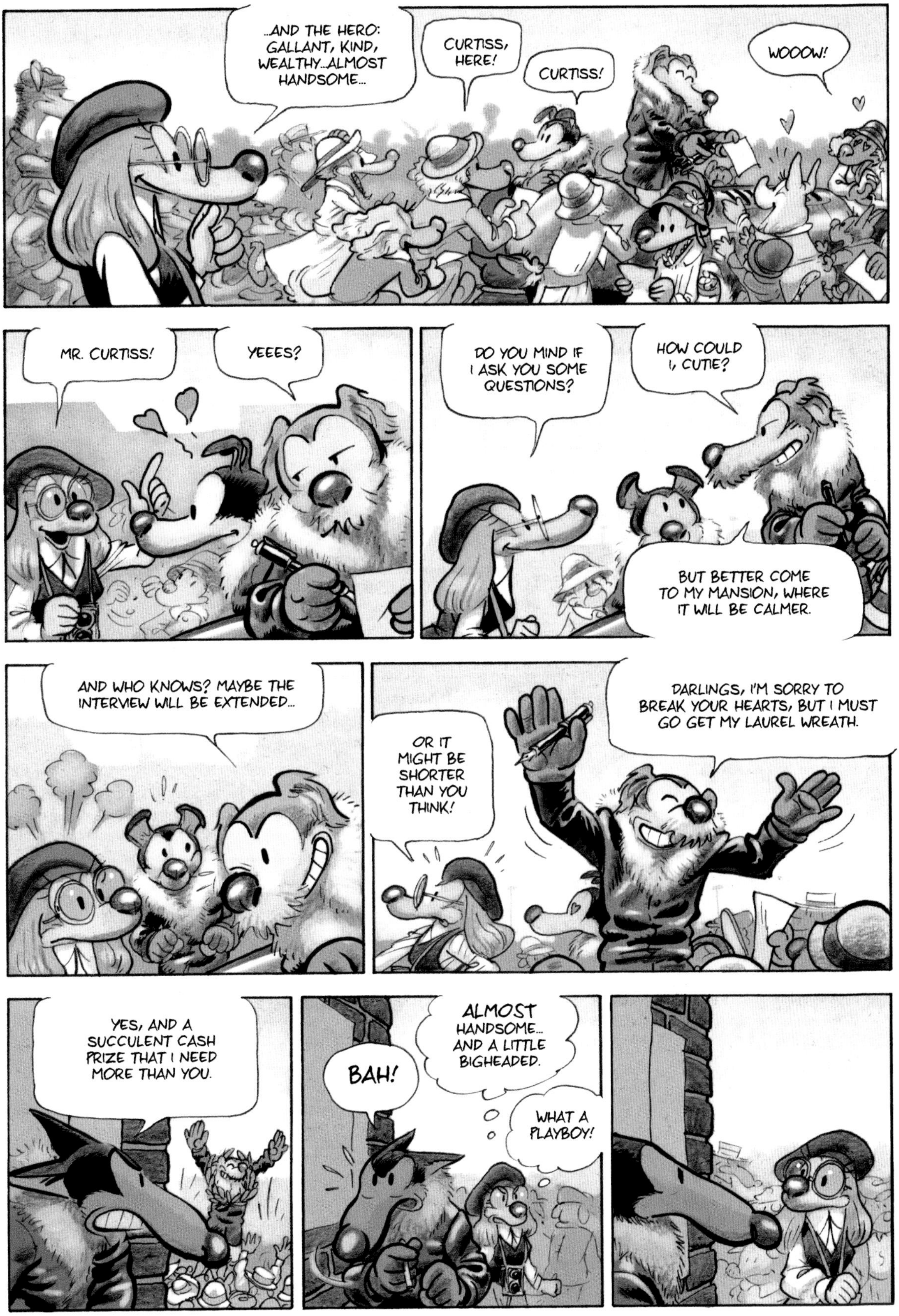
...AND THE HERO: GALLANT, KIND, WEALTHY...ALMOST HANDSOME...
CURTISS, HERE!
CURTISS!
WOOOW!
MR. CURTISS!
YEEES?
DO YOU MIND IF I ASK YOU SOME QUESTIONS?
HOW COULD I, CUTIE?
BUT BETTER COME TO MY MANSION, WHERE IT WILL BE CALMER.
AND WHO KNOWS? MAYBE THE INTERVIEW WILL BE EXTENDED...
OR IT MIGHT BE SHORTER THAN YOU THINK!
DARLINGS, I'M SORRY TO BREAK YOUR HEARTS, BUT I MUST GO GET MY LAUREL WREATH.
YES, AND A SUCCULENT CASH PRIZE THAT I NEED MORE THAN YOU.
BAH!
ALMOST HANDSOME... AND A LITTLE BIGHEADED.
WHAT A PLAYBOY!

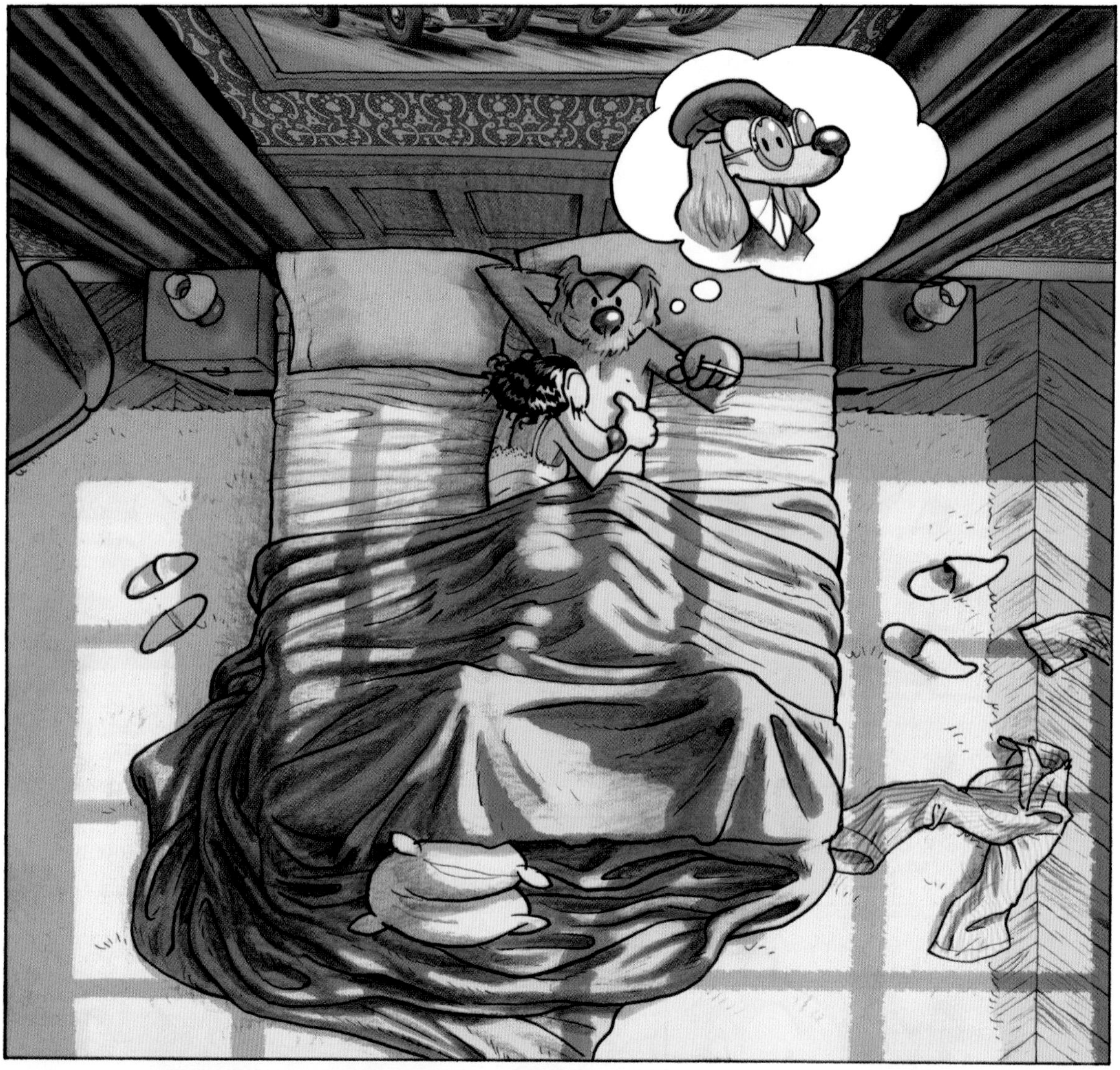

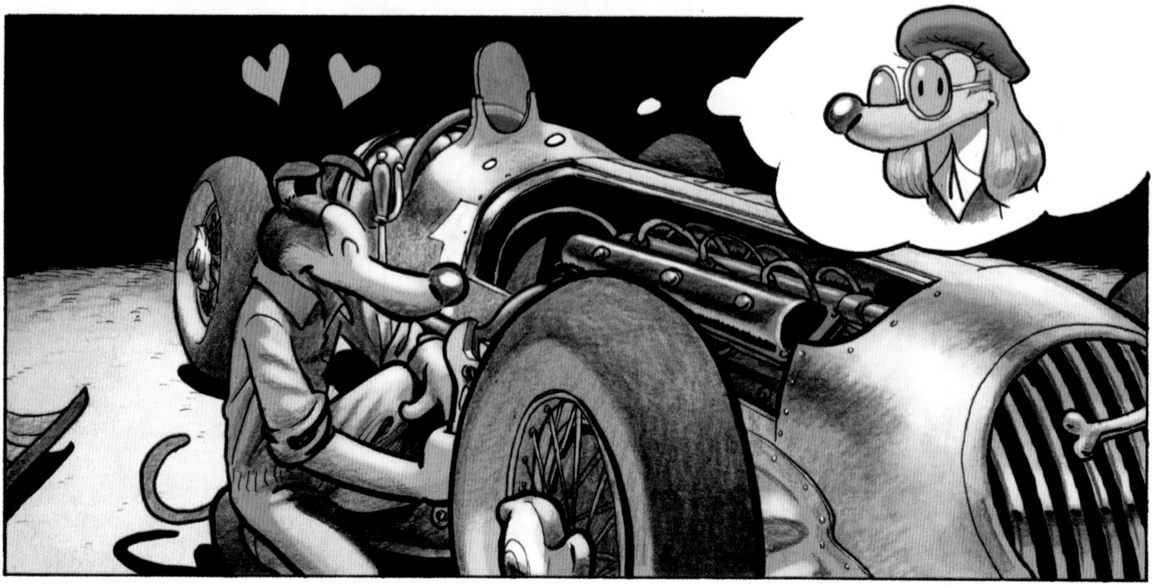

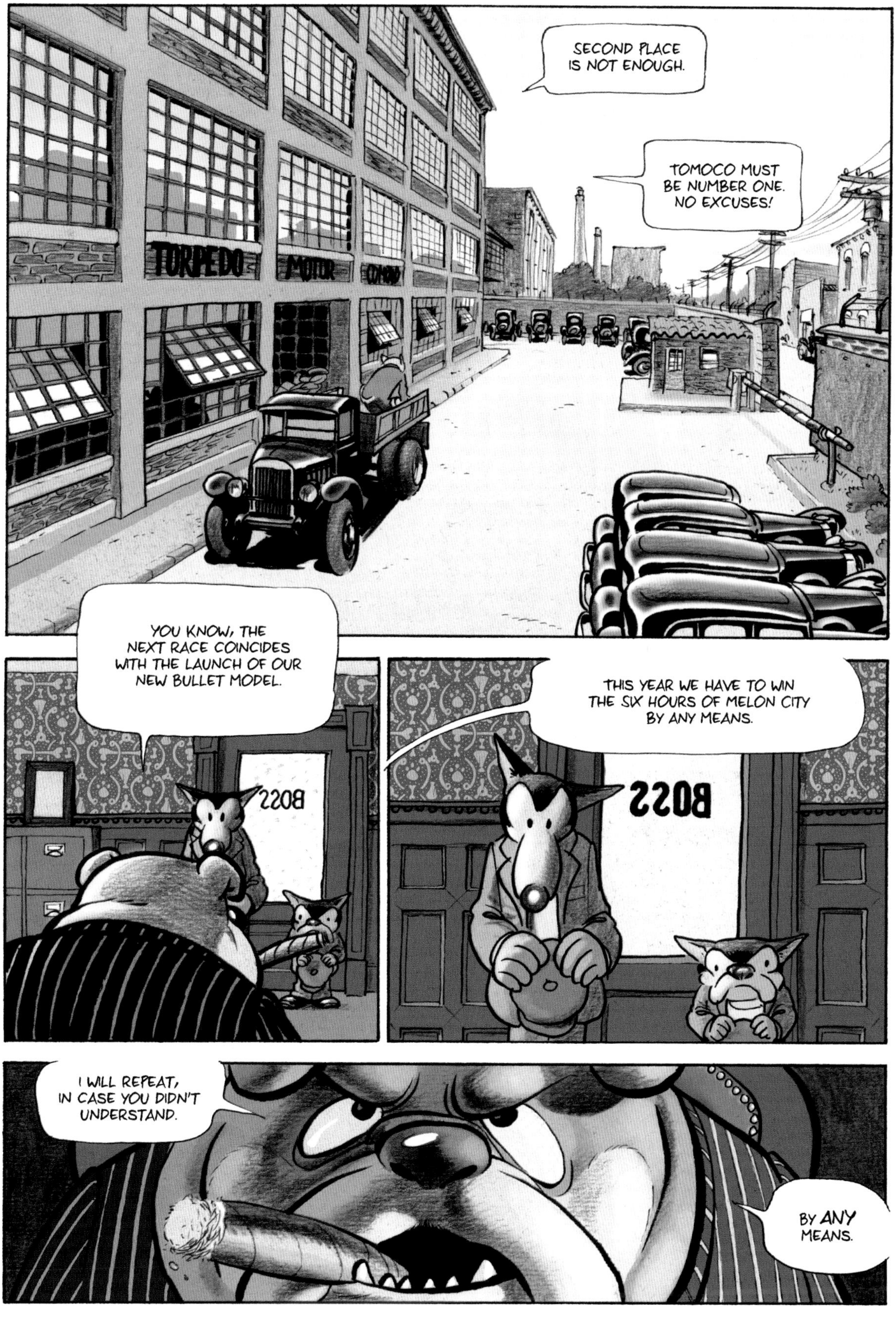
TORPEDO MOTOR COMPANY
SECOND PLACE IS NOT ENOUGH.
TOMOCO MUST BE NUMBER ONE. NO EXCUSES!
YOU KNOW, THE NEXT RACE COINCIDES WITH THE LAUNCH OF OUR NEW BULLET MODEL.
BOSS
THIS YEAR WE HAVE TO WIN THE SIX HOURS OF MELON CITY BY ANY MEANS.
I WILL REPEAT, IN CASE YOU DIDN'T UNDERSTAND.
BY ANY MEANS.

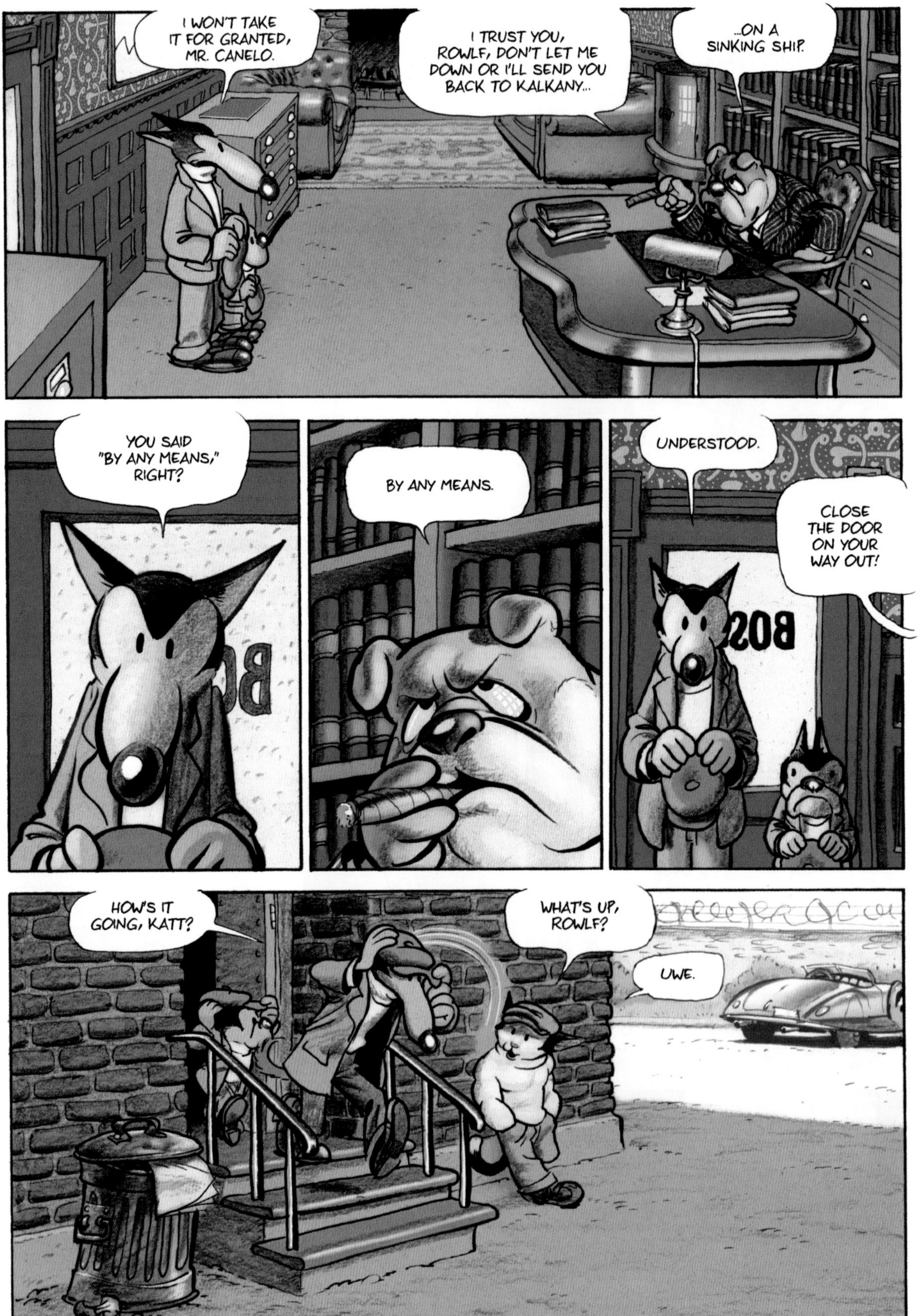
I WON'T TAKE IT FOR GRANTED, MR. CANELO.
I TRUST YOU, ROWLF, DON'T LET ME DOWN OR I'LL SEND YOU BACK TO KALKANY...
...ON A SINKING SHIP.
YOU SAID "BY ANY MEANS," RIGHT?
BY ANY MEANS.
UNDERSTOOD.
CLOSE THE DOOR ON YOUR WAY OUT!
BOS
HOW'S IT GOING, KATT?
WHAT'S UP, ROWLF?
UWE.

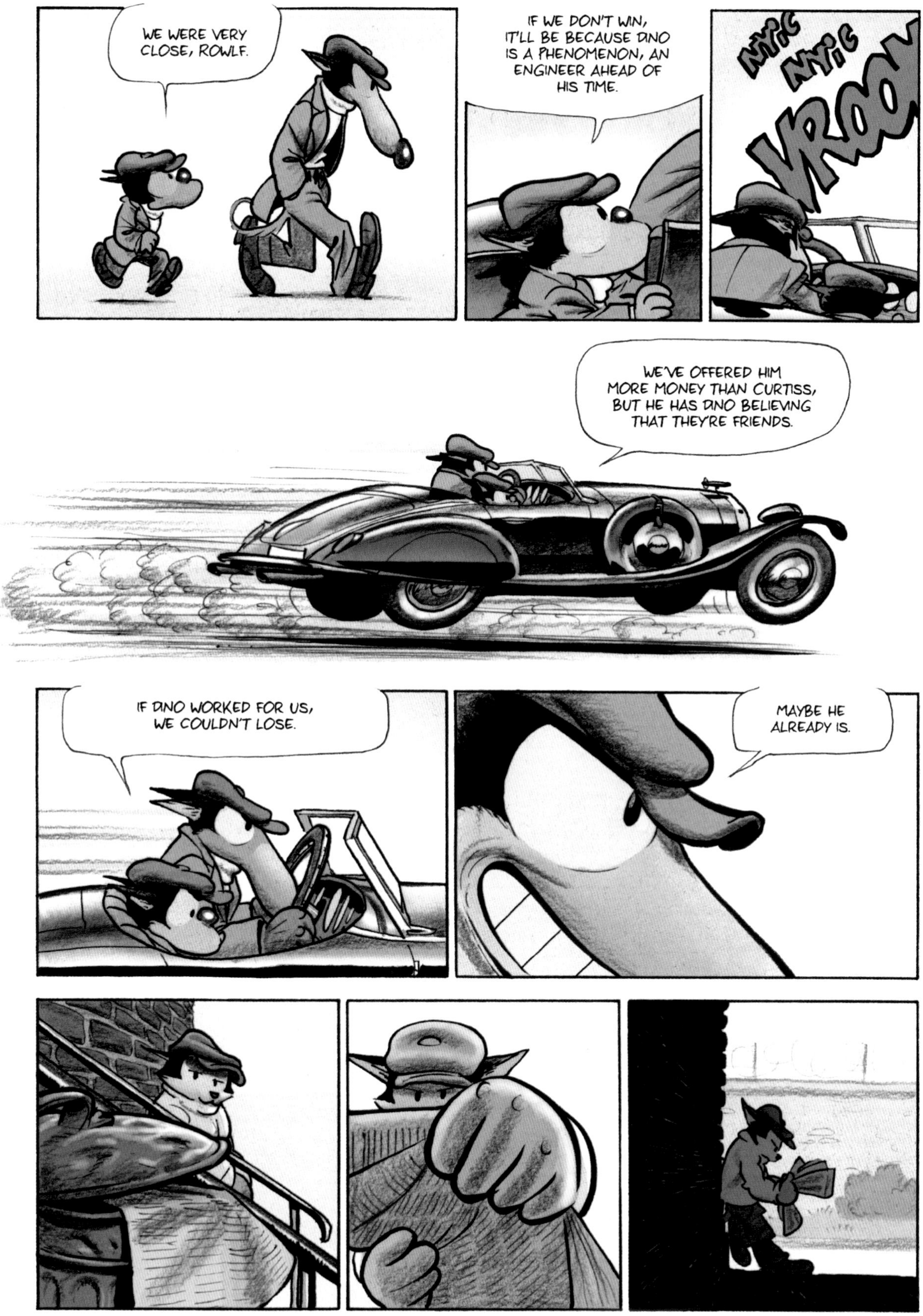
WE WERE VERY CLOSE, ROWLF.
IF WE DON'T WIN, IT'LL BE BECAUSE DINO IS A PHENOMENON, AN ENGINEER AHEAD OF HIS TIME.
NYIG NYIG VROO
WE'VE OFFERED HIM MORE MONEY THAN CURTISS, BUT HE HAS DINO BELIEVING THAT THEY'RE FRIENDS.
IF DINO WORKED FOR US, WE COULDN'T LOSE.
MAYBE HE ALREADY IS.

New advances from scientists: "The sheep explode upon dying"

Escapula News

"Squid that falls asleep, and the current takes it" Interview with the famous publisher of Escapula comics.

The oldest newspaper of the Escapular press. Melon City news every day

Edition n° 3,486   All rights reserved   Melon City, Monday, October 3, 1936   "Not for much getting up early, wake up earlier"   Price: 75 ¢

Curtiss Hill, winner of the Grand Prix "Hot Dog"

The famous pilot dog will donate the award to the foundation "Save Our Cubs" charity for homeless puppies

Curtiss Hill celebrates another triumph on the difficult track of Melon City.

One more year has been celebrated in the mythical circuit of Melon City, the most anticipated test of time, once again it has been the famous dog pilot Curtiss Hill who has risen with the triumph in a race that it has not been without incident. At noon they received the green traffic light and before the first corner Zeichner got in the lead, closely followed by his eternal rival Curtiss Hill, who with a masterful maneuver continued to sneak inside, lo-grando take the lead, a position that he would no longer abandon to the finish line.

"Rowlf is a great rival, it is what makes my victories have more merit "

But Curtiss is not only a great-goalkeeper for his victories. His way to win, always with honesty and chivalry has earned him admiration of most of the animals, especially the females. Without a doubt, the charisma of a champion who after winning with all justice on the track, is able to praise his rivals, in a gesture that only enlarges his legend. At the end of the race, Curtiss did not hesitate to define his maximum rival as an excellent pilot and great athlete. In third position, three laps after the winner, the debutant Smith, who had marked the worst time in qualifying arrived. A rosary of abandonments marked this race, some breakdowns, others by departure from the track, tons of blown tires. Definitely the most spectacular accident was the one starring Owen when he was threatening the second place position of Rowlf Zeichner.

The madness of racing

One more year a great crowd has come together in the Melon City circuit to see the magic of car racing. The heroes of the people are animals that are not afraid of death at the controls of hellishly fast and difficult to control machines, some automobiles with which only mortals can dream that, if they are lucky they will be able to afford have a bicycle. The deafening noise deceiver of the beasts of the asphalt seems to return the animals to times when giant beasts were always on the lookout, and pilots are the hunters who kept it all under control.

Will probably debut a new prototype in the 500 miles of Escapula

It is heard, it is commented in the pit lane, or maybe it's more of a wish than a reality, that Curtiss Hill might be thinking of retiring his mount and exchange for an even more powerful and aerodynamic one. No doubt that it would be a blow to ToMoCo, who already has difficulties in following the pilot to earn some prestige for the brand. Definitely also, the great engineer from Hill is capable of that and more. Will ToMoCo be able to resist it?

WINDS OF WAR IN THE CONTINENT

It is already more than a rumor, they hear the sound of a thunderstorm whose consequences are difficult to foresee. Industries work on all machines and imports of such grow without ceasing. This provokes threats and the threats are no longer veiled. Barely a generation has passed but it seems that they have already forgotten the consequences of war. Hopefully the leaders of the countries of the continent reconsider before it is too late, although we are pessimistic: The history books tell us that in times of economic crisis, the population tends to think you don't have much to lose and only something to gain in an armed conflict.

Unstoppable rise of Pitbulism in Kalkany

Neighboring coun threaten with dec if the murders of the Calcanean co not stop.

The rise of pitbulism, stemmed from economic impoverishment and culture of the calcaneus nation, has caused the mass exodus of many who flee from the massacres that, they claim, by gangs out of control. Or maybe controlled by the Government, they claim.

Rowlf Zeichner:

"The car engine of Curtiss is a lot more powerful"

The calcaneus pilot Rowlf Zeichner has passed, in a short time, from being a stranger to privileged positions in podiums from the last races.
An ambitious pilot, who does not settle with less than victory. Torpedo Motor Company has seen in him the dog that can kill Curtiss Hill's supremacy in the races. The President of ToMoCo does not ignore the great advertising value and spares no expense to get it. In Zeichner, he has found an ally who not only does not seem to be afraid of death, but also an ambition that knows no limits. However, to the sponsors Zeichner has quite weak limits. Though he is of strong character, he is a bad loser, and generally spreads the blame for his defeats right and left. He does the company, who pays his salary, a disservice, speaking poorly of the quality and reliability of the vehicles it manufactures and markets for sale.

"There was oil on the Pista, we were about to crash."

In recent times, controversy surrounds him with suspi-cions of some rivals—and also of a sector of the public. Some believe the accidents could be coincidences, however, and it is too soon to talk about sabotage or accusations of such gravity. At the moment there has not been any proof showing a link between such accidents and the ToMoCo pilot. Zeichner's excuses for not having achieved the triumph in the test range from oil on the track to trouble with the change.

"There was a problem with the change, I had to do the whole race in third."

Still, Zeichner has a faithful legion of followers, who admirehim for never throwing in the towel. Sport and sportsmanship do not count a lot for them, only victory, and if he wins it hardly matters how it was done.
Curtiss Hill and Rowlf Zeichner, two opposite ways of understanding the competition. We will not be those who take sides, that is up to you. We we will continue to inform with the impartiality that characterizes us.

Owen is still hospitalized and will not be able to dispute the 500 miles of Escapula

Owen, the pilot who suffered a spectacular accident when contesting second place of Rowlf Zeichner's was hospitalized after suffering the fracture of several bones. Although not grave, a long recovery of at least forty days awaits due to the funnel that has been placed on his neck. His co-pilot miraculously came out unharmed after being thrown and falling on some bushes.
This mishap will set them back of the competition for a while and they have already ruled out their participation in the 500 miles of Escapula, the most important race of the season. We will miss you, Owen!

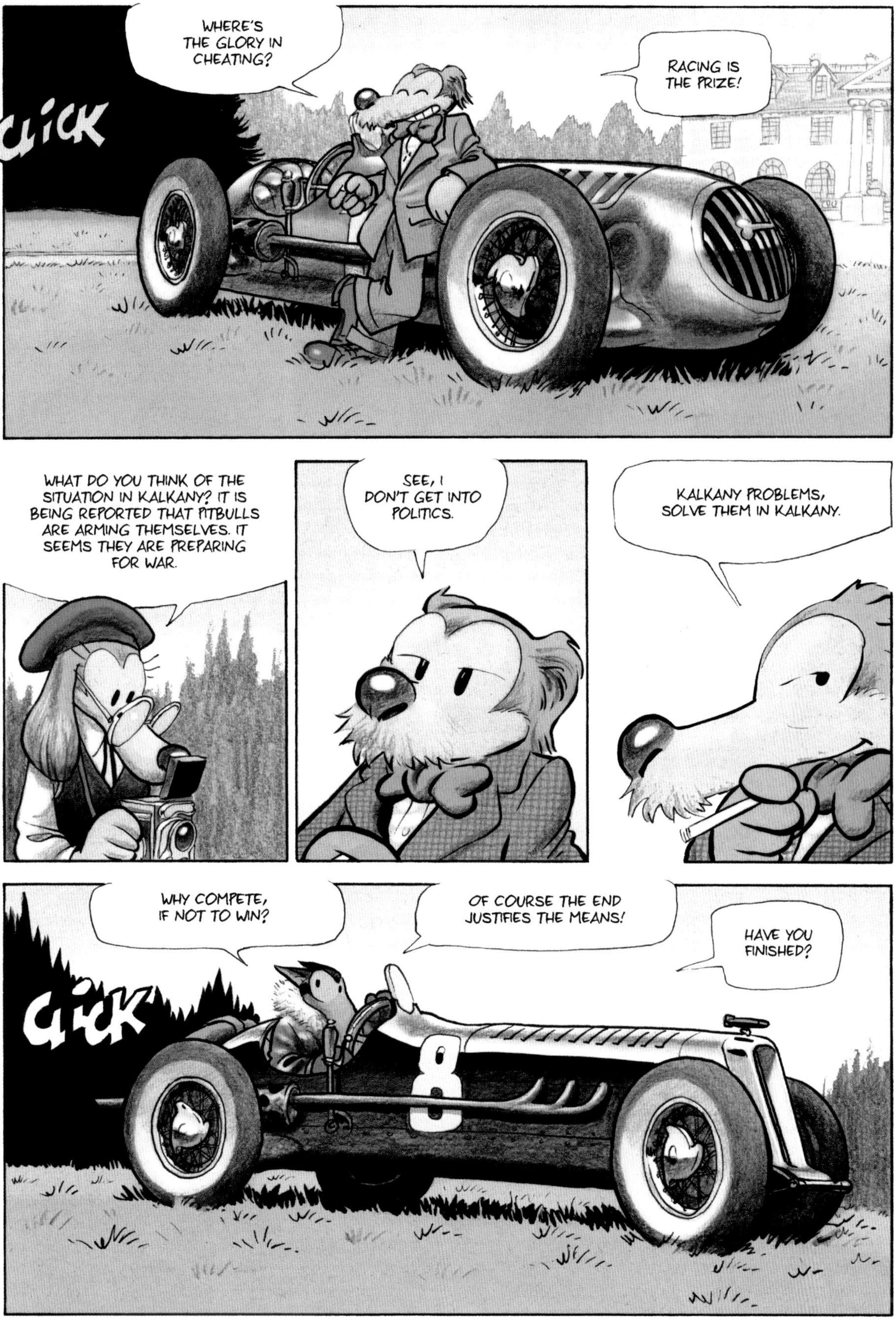
WHERE'S THE GLORY IN CHEATING?
CLICK
RACING IS THE PRIZE!
WHAT DO YOU THINK OF THE SITUATION IN KALKANY? IT IS BEING REPORTED THAT PITBULLS ARE ARMING THEMSELVES. IT SEEMS THEY ARE PREPARING FOR WAR.
SEE, I DON'T GET INTO POLITICS.
KALKANY PROBLEMS, SOLVE THEM IN KALKANY.
WHY COMPETE, IF NOT TO WIN?
OF COURSE THE END JUSTIFIES THE MEANS!
CLICK
HAVE YOU FINISHED?
8

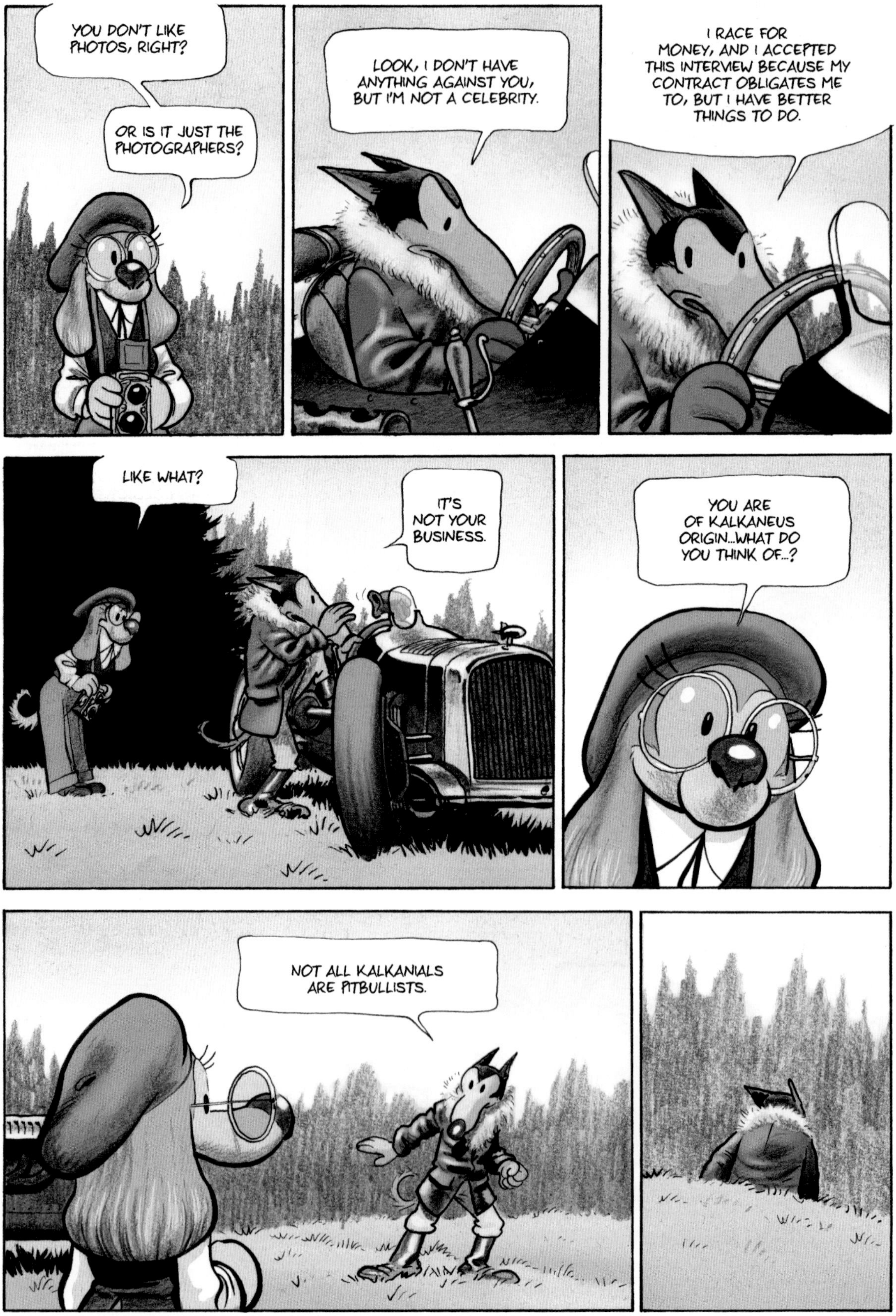
YOU DON'T LIKE PHOTOS, RIGHT?
OR IS IT JUST THE PHOTOGRAPHERS?
LOOK, I DON'T HAVE ANYTHING AGAINST YOU, BUT I'M NOT A CELEBRITY.
I RACE FOR MONEY, AND I ACCEPTED THIS INTERVIEW BECAUSE MY CONTRACT OBLIGATES ME TO, BUT I HAVE BETTER THINGS TO DO.
LIKE WHAT?
IT'S NOT YOUR BUSINESS.
YOU ARE OF KALKANEUS ORIGIN...WHAT DO YOU THINK OF...?
NOT ALL KALKANIALS ARE PITBULLISTS.

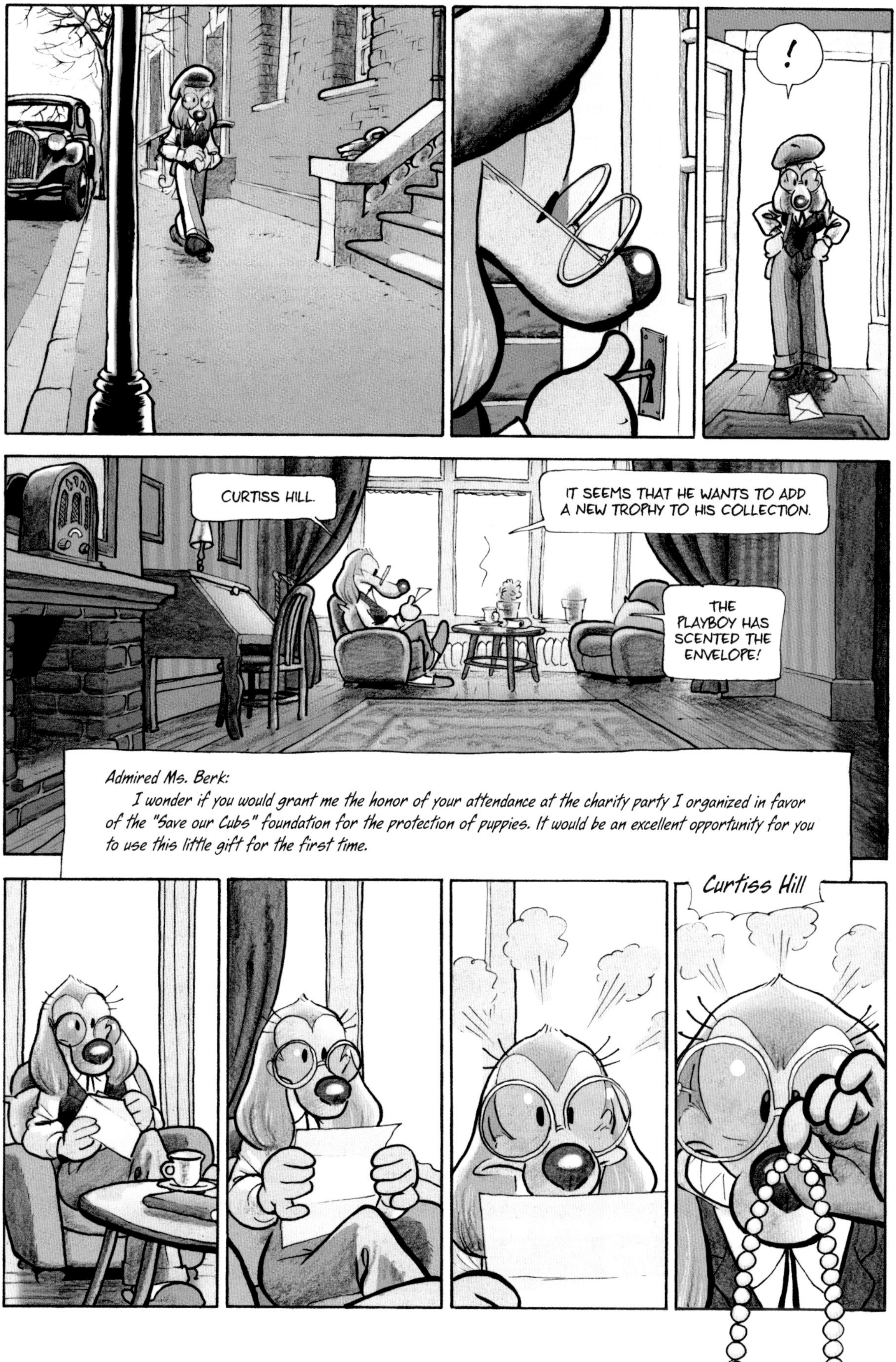
!
CURTISS HILL.
IT SEEMS THAT HE WANTS TO ADD A NEW TROPHY TO HIS COLLECTION.
THE PLAYBOY HAS SCENTED THE ENVELOPE!
Admired Ms. Berk:
I wonder if you would grant me the honor of your attendance at the charity party I organized in favor of the "Save our Cubs" foundation for the protection of puppies. It would be an excellent opportunity for you to use this little gift for the first time.
Curtiss Hill

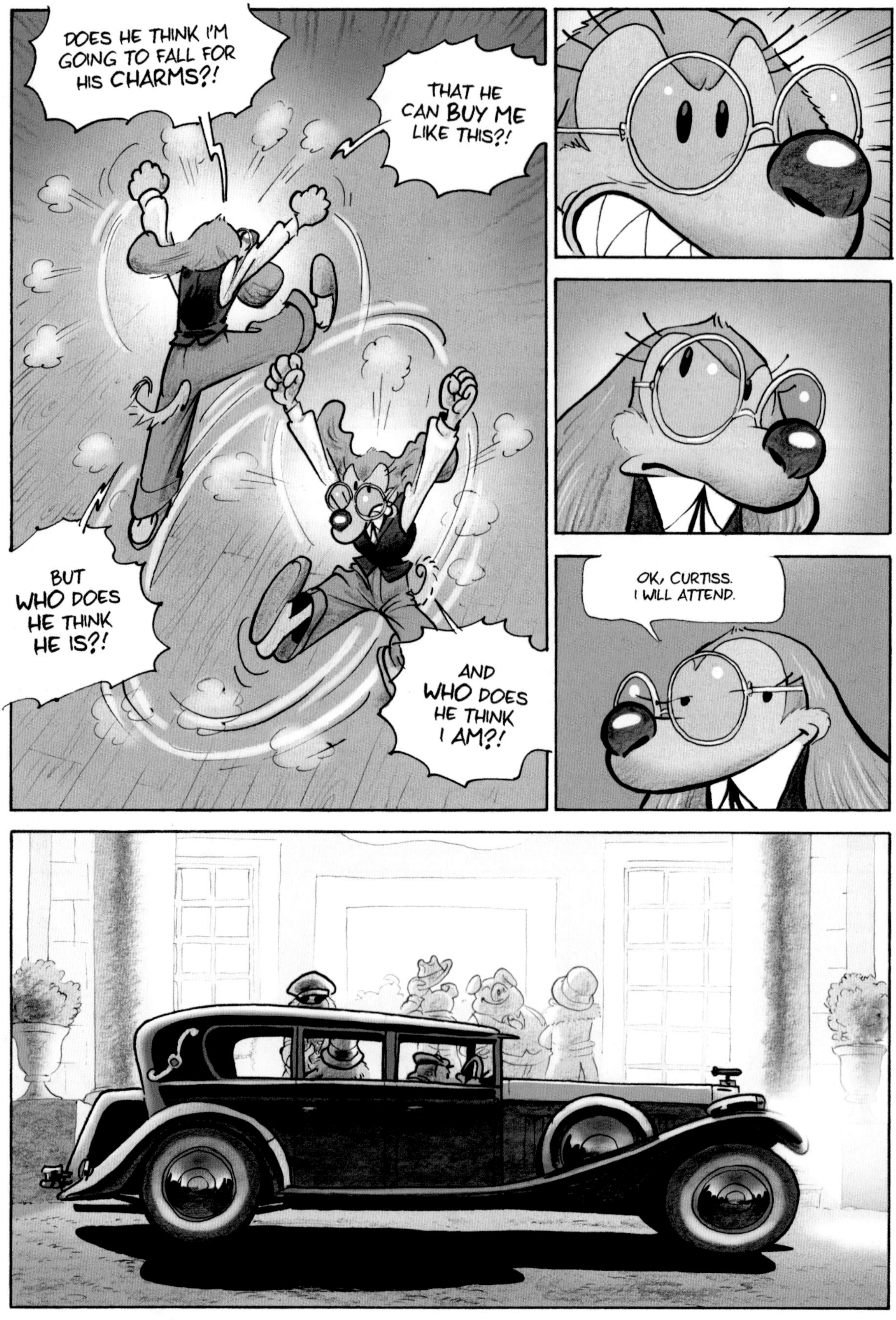
DOES HE THINK I'M GOING TO FALL FOR HIS CHARMS?!
THAT HE CAN BUY ME LIKE THIS?!
BUT WHO DOES HE THINK HE IS?!
AND WHO DOES HE THINK I AM?!
OK, CURTISS. I WILL ATTEND.

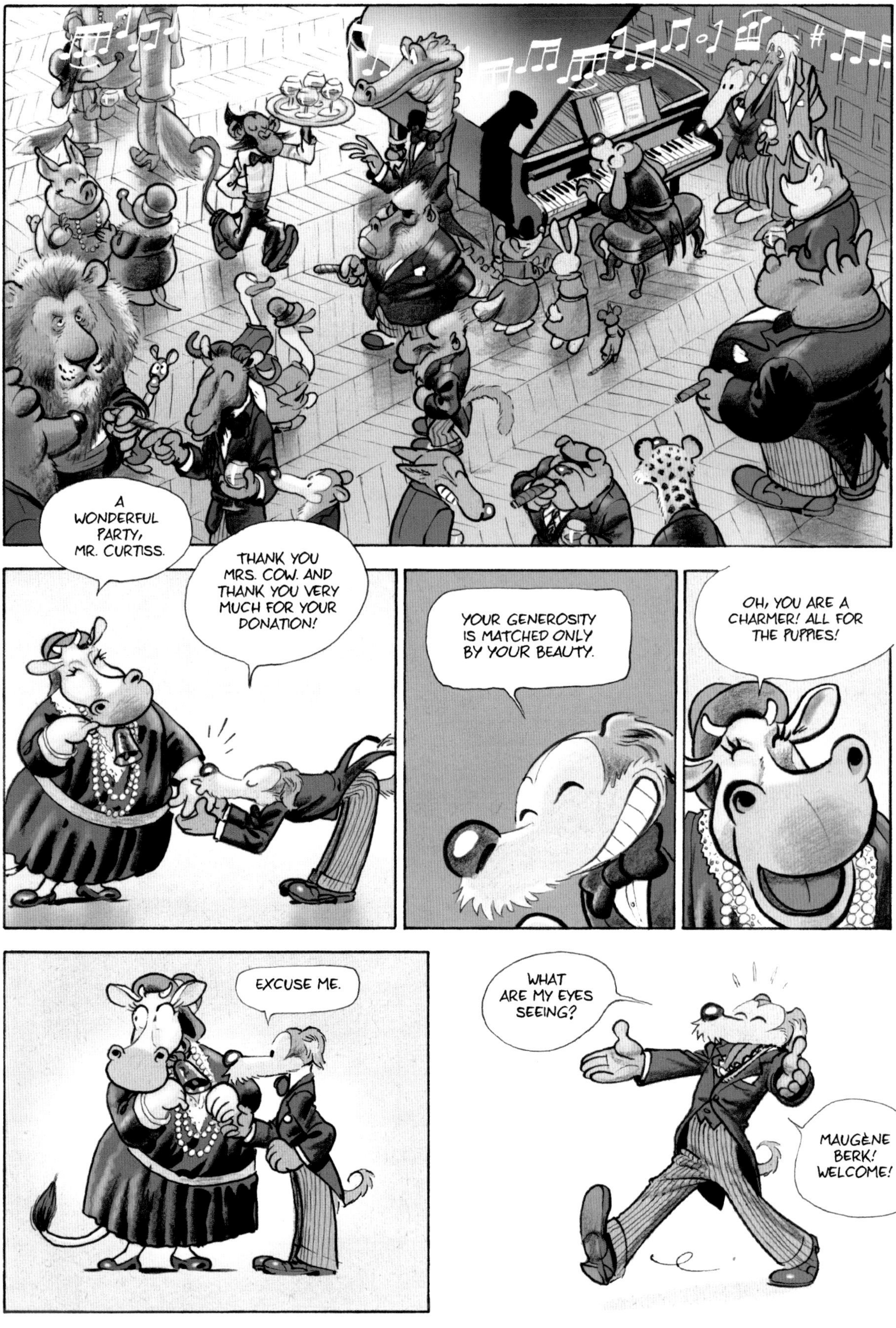
A WONDERFUL PARTY, MR. CURTISS.
THANK YOU MRS. COW. AND THANK YOU VERY MUCH FOR YOUR DONATION!
YOUR GENEROSITY IS MATCHED ONLY BY YOUR BEAUTY.
OH, YOU ARE A CHARMER! ALL FOR THE PUPPIES!
EXCUSE ME.
WHAT ARE MY EYES SEEING?
MAUGÈNE BERK! WELCOME!

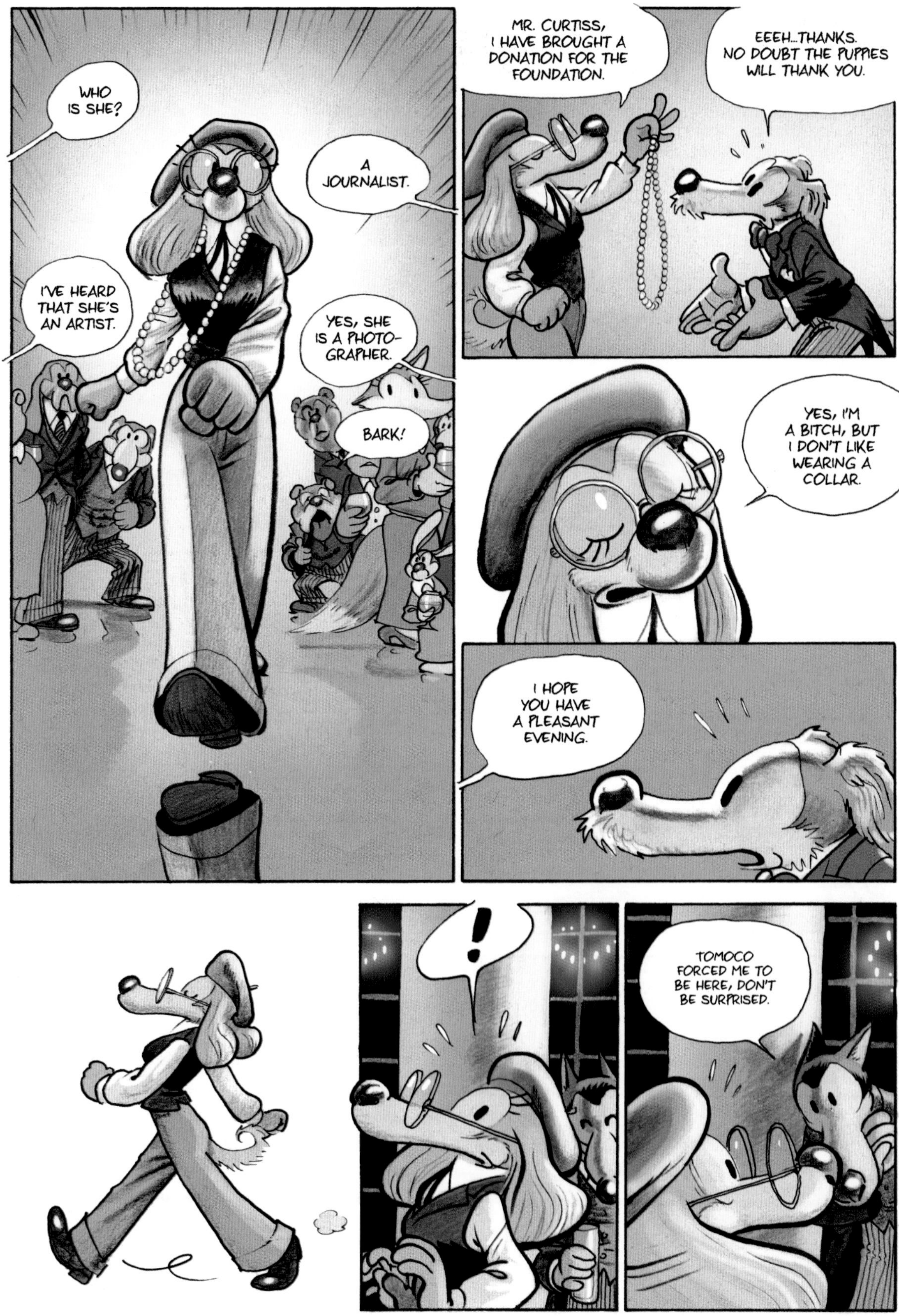
WHO IS SHE?
A JOURNALIST.
I'VE HEARD THAT SHE'S AN ARTIST.
YES, SHE IS A PHOTOGRAPHER.
BARK!
MR. CURTISS, I HAVE BROUGHT A DONATION FOR THE FOUNDATION.
EEEH...THANKS. NO DOUBT THE PUPPIES WILL THANK YOU.
YES, I'M A BITCH, BUT I DON'T LIKE WEARING A COLLAR.
I HOPE YOU HAVE A PLEASANT EVENING.
!
TOMOCO FORCED ME TO BE HERE, DON'T BE SURPRISED.

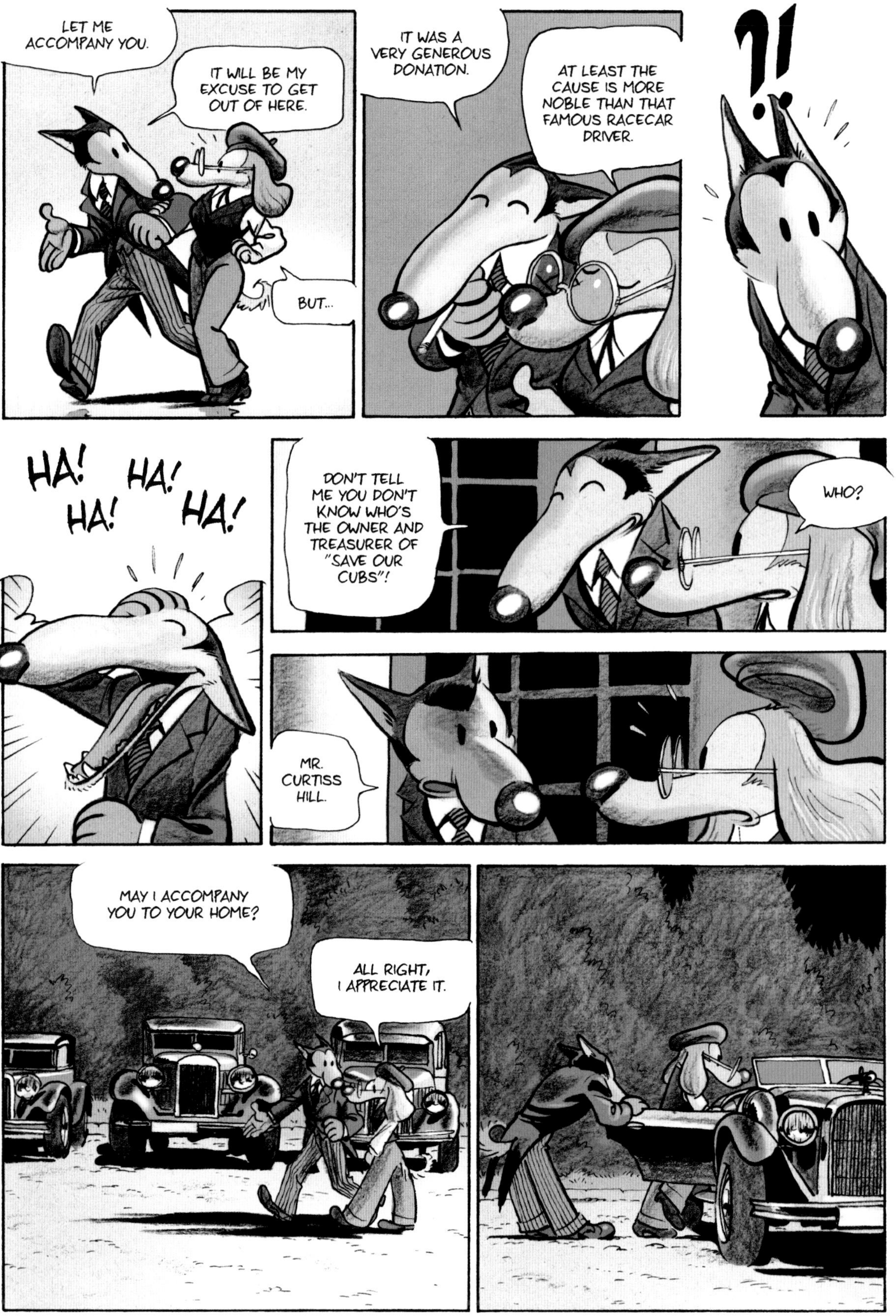

LET ME ACCOMPANY YOU.
IT WILL BE MY EXCUSE TO GET OUT OF HERE.
BUT...
IT WAS A VERY GENEROUS DONATION.
AT LEAST THE CAUSE IS MORE NOBLE THAN THAT FAMOUS RACECAR DRIVER.
?!
HA! HA! HA! HA!
DON'T TELL ME YOU DON'T KNOW WHO'S THE OWNER AND TREASURER OF "SAVE OUR CUBS"!
WHO?
MR. CURTISS HILL.
MAY I ACCOMPANY YOU TO YOUR HOME?
ALL RIGHT, I APPRECIATE IT.

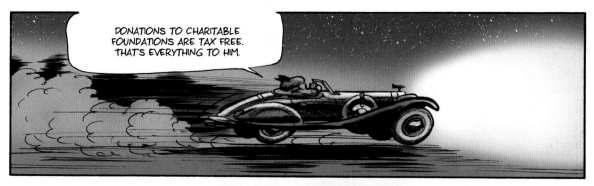

DONATIONS TO CHARITABLE FOUNDATIONS ARE TAX FREE. THAT'S EVERYTHING TO HIM.

AND YOU'VE SEEN WHO THE DONORS ARE: COUNCILORS, THE MAYOR, SENATORS... DON'T YOU THINK IT'S SUSPICIOUS?

DO YOU MEAN THAT...?

LET'S JUST SAY IT'S A WAY TO PAY FOR THE "SERVICES" OFFERED BY CURTISS...

WHAT KIND OF SERVICES?!

I THINK I'VE SAID ENOUGH FOR TODAY. YOU'VE ALREADY SEEN THAT MY BOSS IS ONE OF THE "BENEFACTORS."

SORRY! IT IS NOT MY INTENTION TO PUT YOU IN A COMPROMISING POSITION.

IF YOU STAY TO LIVE IN MELON CITY, YOU WILL FIND OUT FOR YOURSELF.

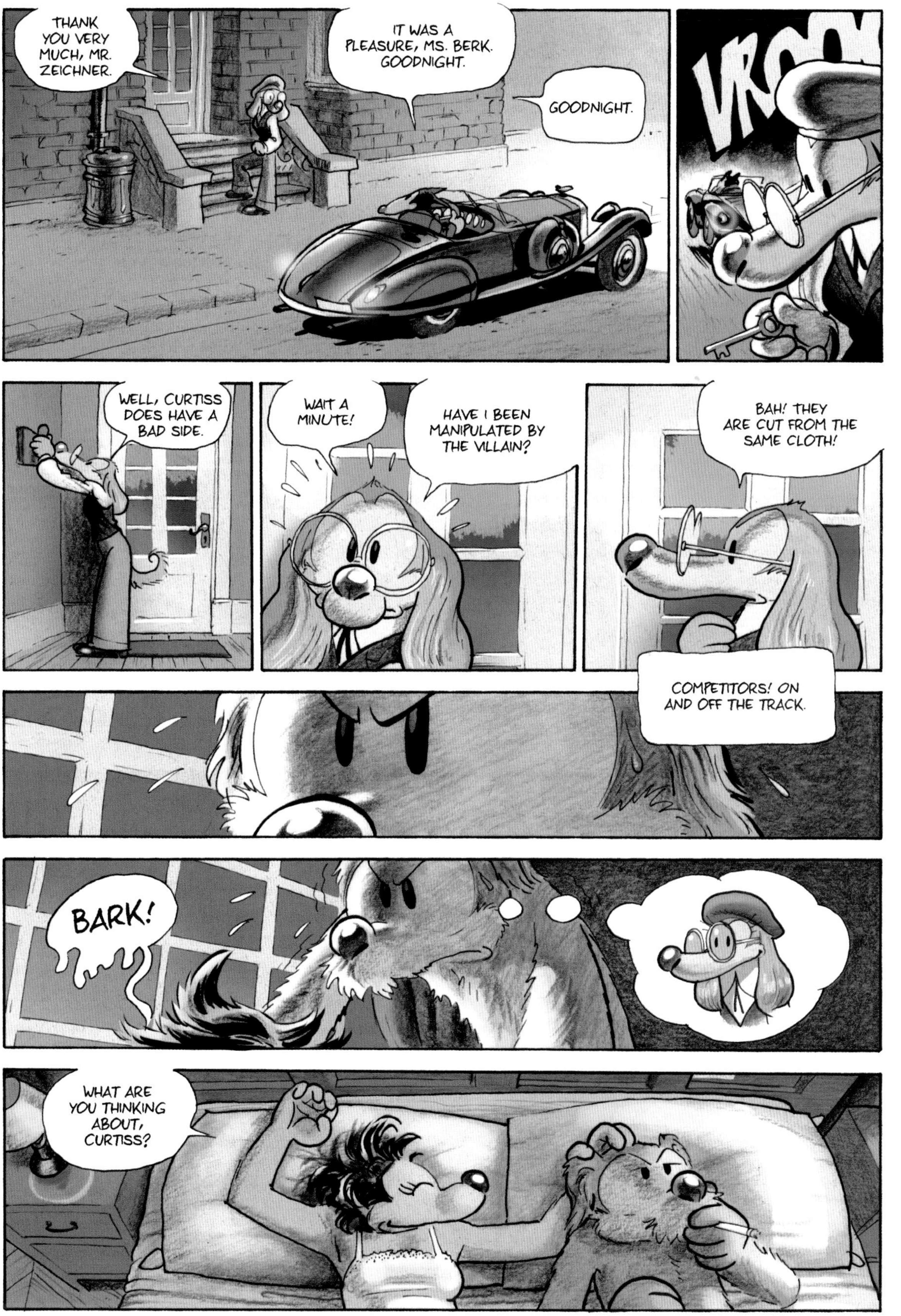
THANK YOU VERY MUCH, MR. ZEICHNER.
IT WAS A PLEASURE, MS. BERK. GOODNIGHT.
GOODNIGHT.
VROO
WELL, CURTISS DOES HAVE A BAD SIDE.
WAIT A MINUTE!
HAVE I BEEN MANIPULATED BY THE VILLAIN?
BAH! THEY ARE CUT FROM THE SAME CLOTH!
COMPETITORS! ON AND OFF THE TRACK.
BARK!
WHAT ARE YOU THINKING ABOUT, CURTISS?

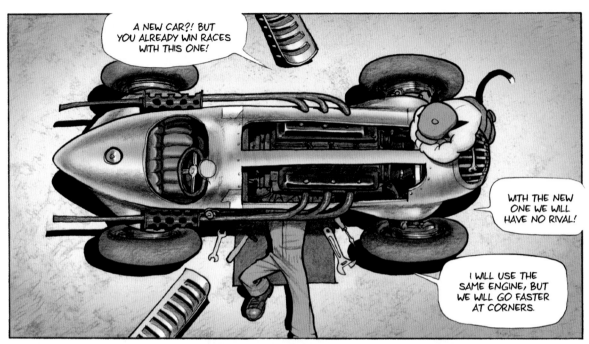

A NEW CAR?! BUT YOU ALREADY WIN RACES WITH THIS ONE!

WITH THE NEW ONE WE WILL HAVE NO RIVAL!

I WILL USE THE SAME ENGINE, BUT WE WILL GO FASTER AT CORNERS.

AND HOW WILL YOU GET IT TO DO THAT?

YOU'LL SEE!

IT WILL BE MY MASTERPIECE.

AND LATER, I PLAN TO BUILD A "SHEEP-EXPLOSION" ENGINE.

IT SOUNDS DANGEROUS.

IT IS! HAVE YOU HEARD FROM YOUR FAMILY IN KALKANY?

NOT FOR WEEKS.

I HOPE THERE WON'T BE WAR.

WHO KNOWS IF WAR CAN BE THEIR SALVATION...

THE PITBULLS ARE EXTERMINATING THE CATS IN KALKANY AND NOBODY IS DOING ANYTHING TO STOP IT.

WHAT DO YOU MEAN, EXTERMINATING?

THEY ARE ARRESTED FOR NO REASON AND NOBODY SEES THEM AGAIN.

THEY COULD BE IN PRISON.

NO, DINO. THERE ARE WITNESSES.

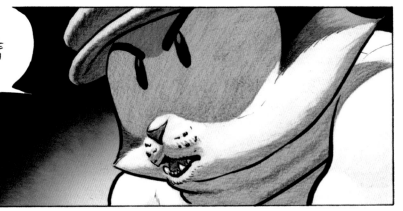

THEY PUT THEM IN CONCENTRATION CAMPS. THEY ENTER THROUGH THE DOOR AND EXIT THROUGH THE CHIMNEYS OF THE CREMATORIUMS.

THAT CAN'T BE!

YES, DINO, IT'S HAPPENING! CATS ARRIVE CLANDESTINELY IN ESCÁPULA, AND ALL OF THEM TELL THE SAME STORY.

SOME PEOPLE WITH MONEY ARE BRINGING REFUGEES IN CARGO BOATS, BUT THAT'S NOT ENOUGH. GOVERNMENTS MUST INTERVENE.

ALTHOUGH I FEAR THAT THE BIG FISH WILL ONLY INTERVENE IF WAR CAN INCREASE THEIR FORTUNES.

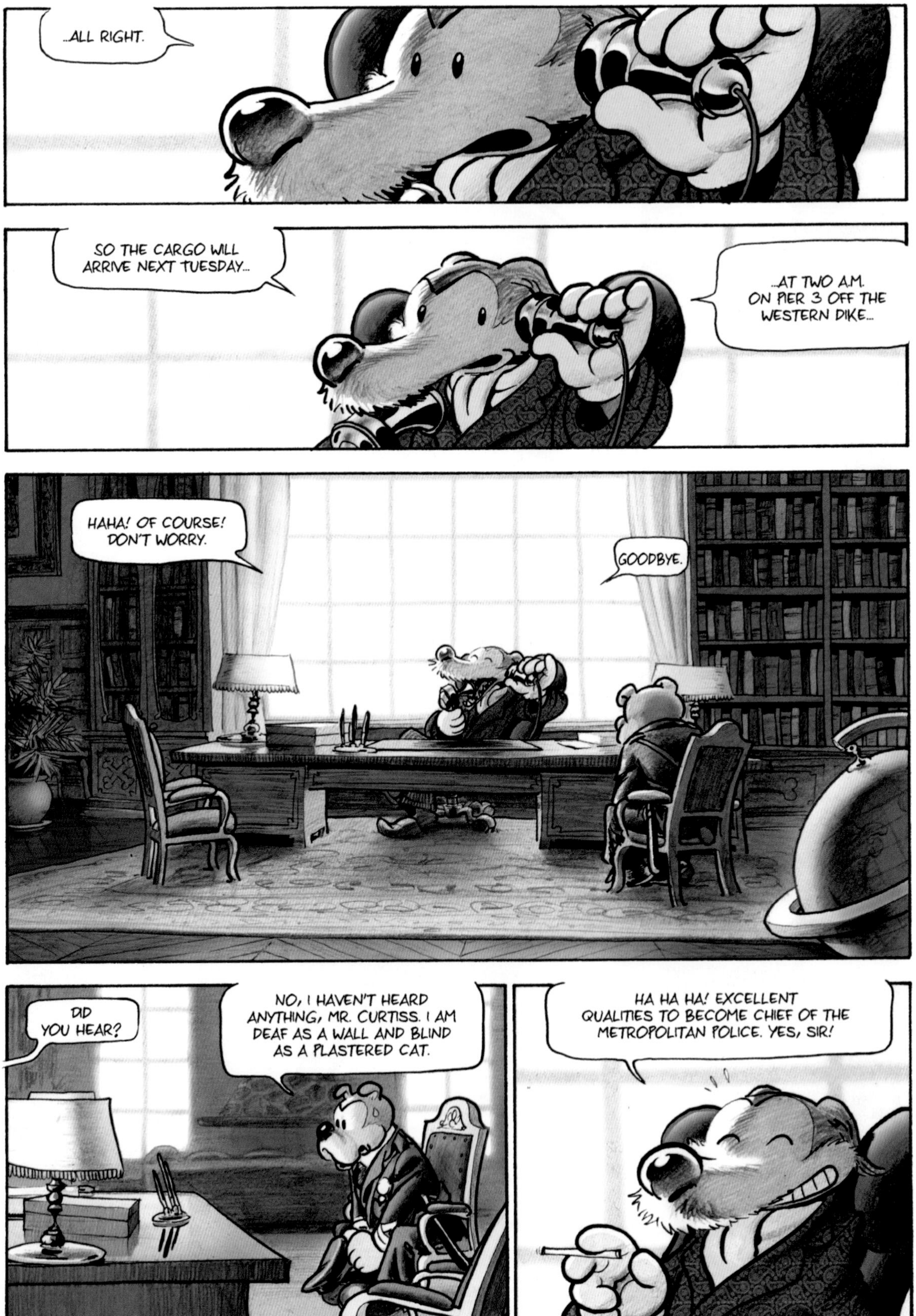
...ALL RIGHT.
SO THE CARGO WILL ARRIVE NEXT TUESDAY...
...AT TWO A.M. ON PIER 3 OFF THE WESTERN DIKE...
HAHA! OF COURSE! DON'T WORRY.
GOODBYE.
DID YOU HEAR?
NO, I HAVEN'T HEARD ANYTHING, MR. CURTISS. I AM DEAF AS A WALL AND BLIND AS A PLASTERED CAT.
HA HA HA! EXCELLENT QUALITIES TO BECOME CHIEF OF THE METROPOLITAN POLICE. YES, SIR!

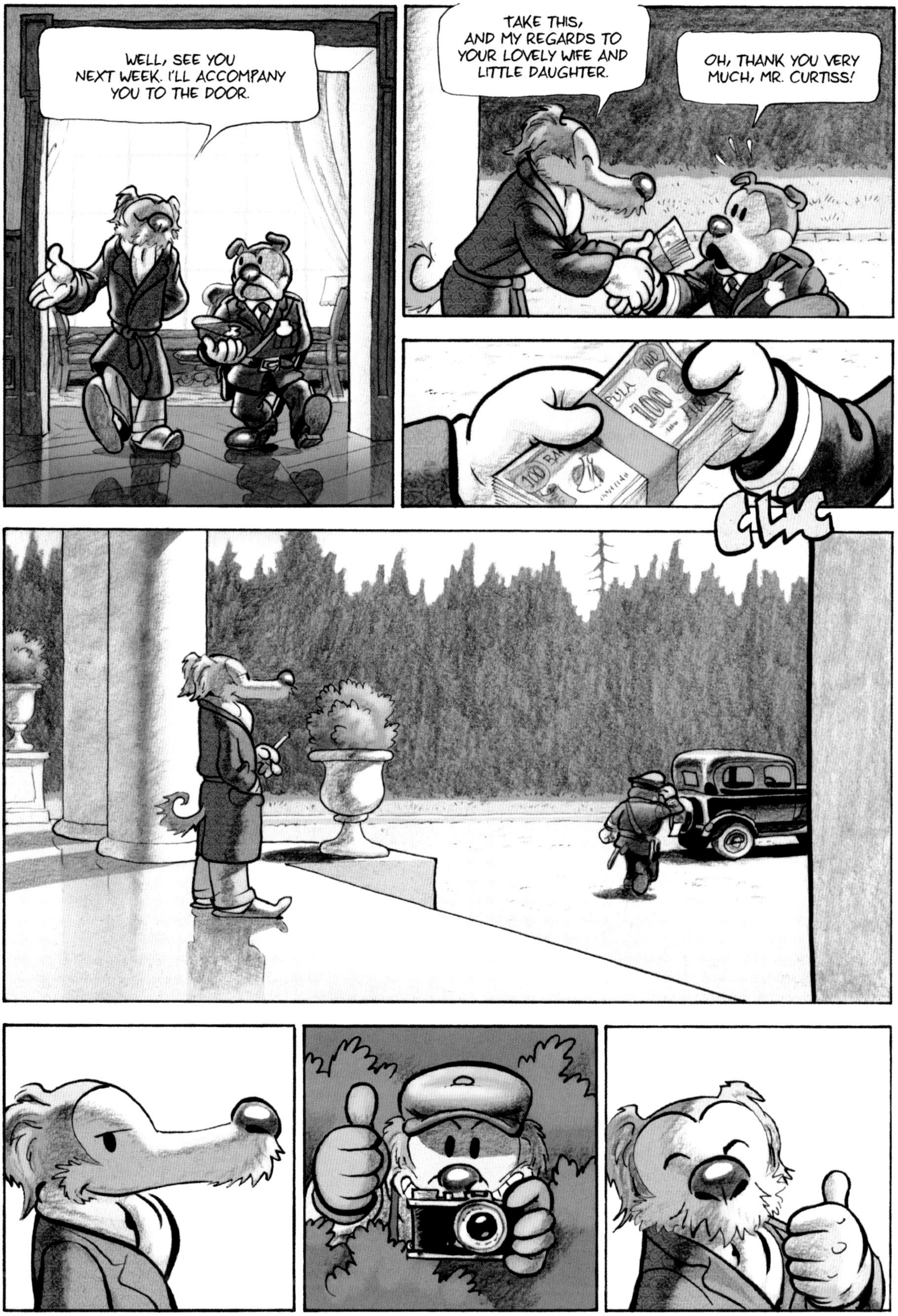
WELL, SEE YOU NEXT WEEK. I'LL ACCOMPANY YOU TO THE DOOR.
TAKE THIS, AND MY REGARDS TO YOUR LOVELY WIFE AND LITTLE DAUGHTER.
OH, THANK YOU VERY MUCH, MR. CURTISS!
CLIC

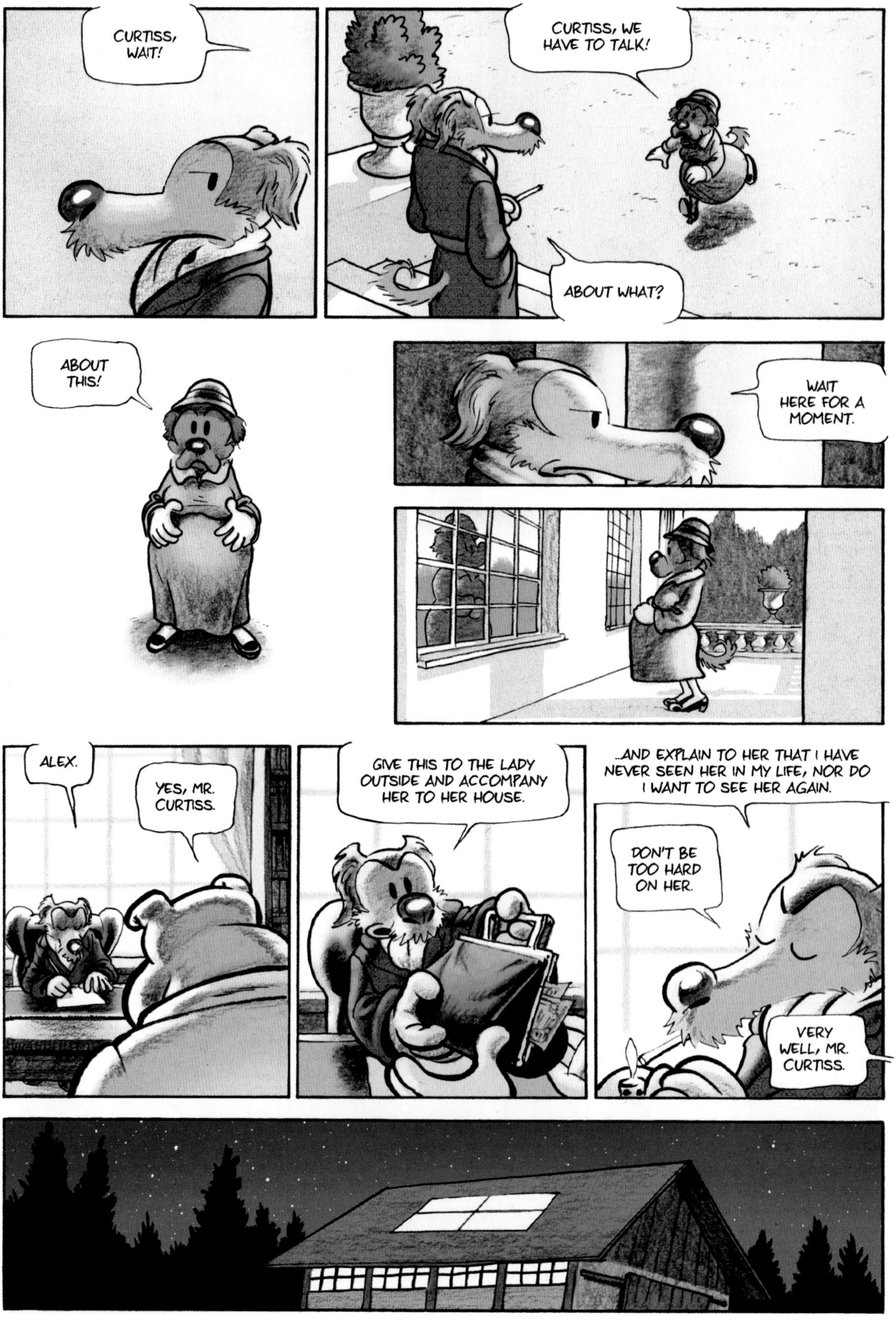
CURTISS, WAIT!
CURTISS, WE HAVE TO TALK!
ABOUT WHAT?
ABOUT THIS!
WAIT HERE FOR A MOMENT.
ALEX.
YES, MR. CURTISS.
GIVE THIS TO THE LADY OUTSIDE AND ACCOMPANY HER TO HER HOUSE.
...AND EXPLAIN TO HER THAT I HAVE NEVER SEEN HER IN MY LIFE, NOR DO I WANT TO SEE HER AGAIN.
DON'T BE TOO HARD ON HER.
VERY WELL, MR. CURTISS.

REAR ENGINE? I DON'T KNOW, IT DOESN'T LOOK VERY GRACEFUL.

WHEN IT STARTS WINNING RACES, EVERYONE WILL SEE HOW BEAUTIFUL IT IS. IT WILL BE THE NEW STANDARD FOR BEAUTY.

THE CENTER OF GRAVITY WILL BE LOWER AND MORE BALANCED.

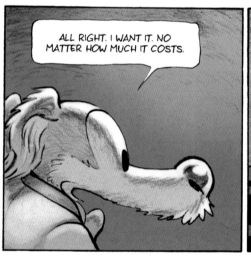

ALL RIGHT. I WANT IT. NO MATTER HOW MUCH IT COSTS.

DO YOU THINK YOU'LL HAVE IT READY FOR THE 500 MILES?

THAT'LL BE VERY DIFFICULT! MAYBE FOR THE NEXT ONE.

IT'S OKAY. LET'S DO IT!

DINO, YOU ARE A GENIUS!

THANK YOU, MR. CURTISS.

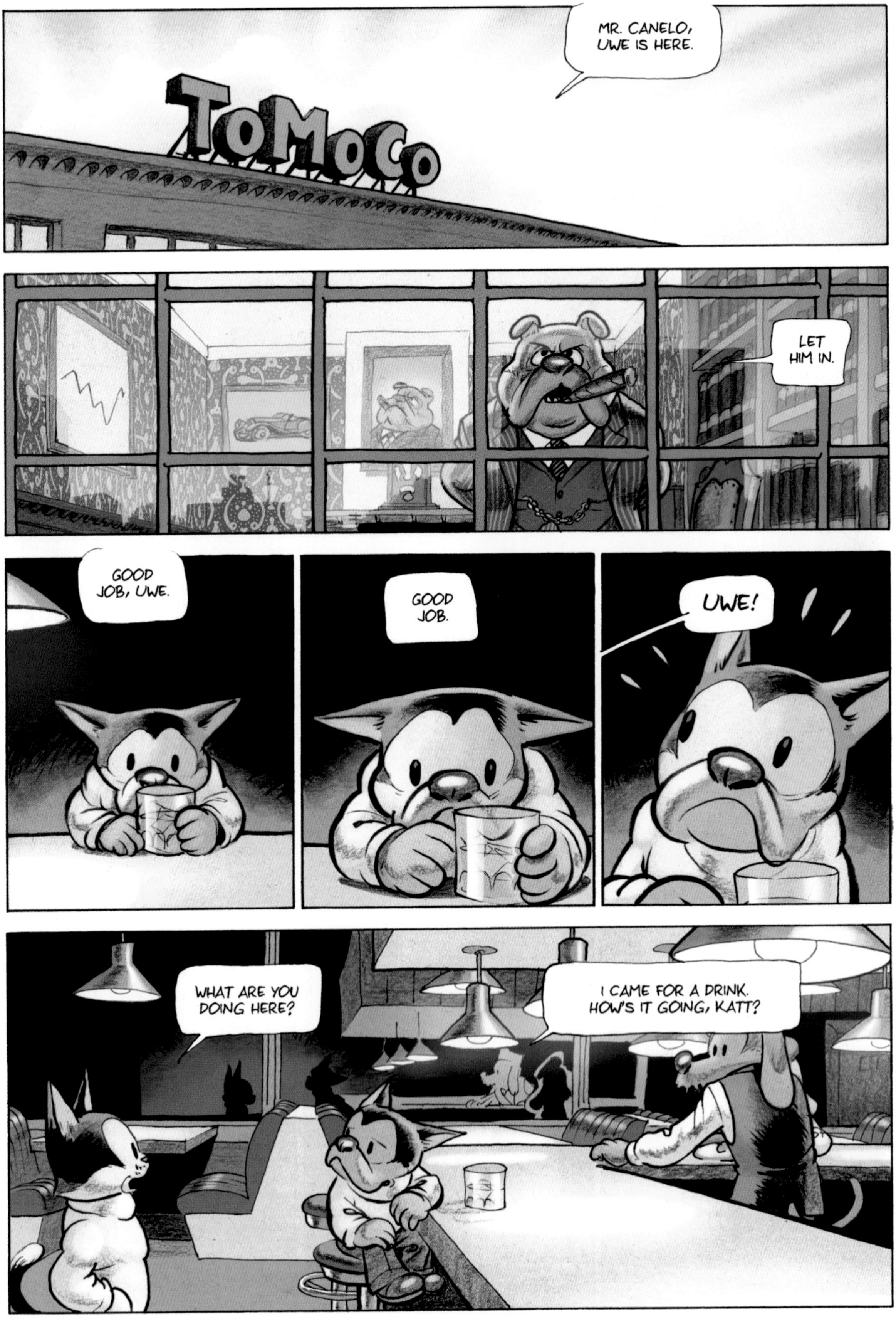
TOMOCO
MR. CANELO, UWE IS HERE.
LET HIM IN.
GOOD JOB, UWE.
GOOD JOB.
UWE!
WHAT ARE YOU DOING HERE?
I CAME FOR A DRINK. HOW'S IT GOING, KATT?

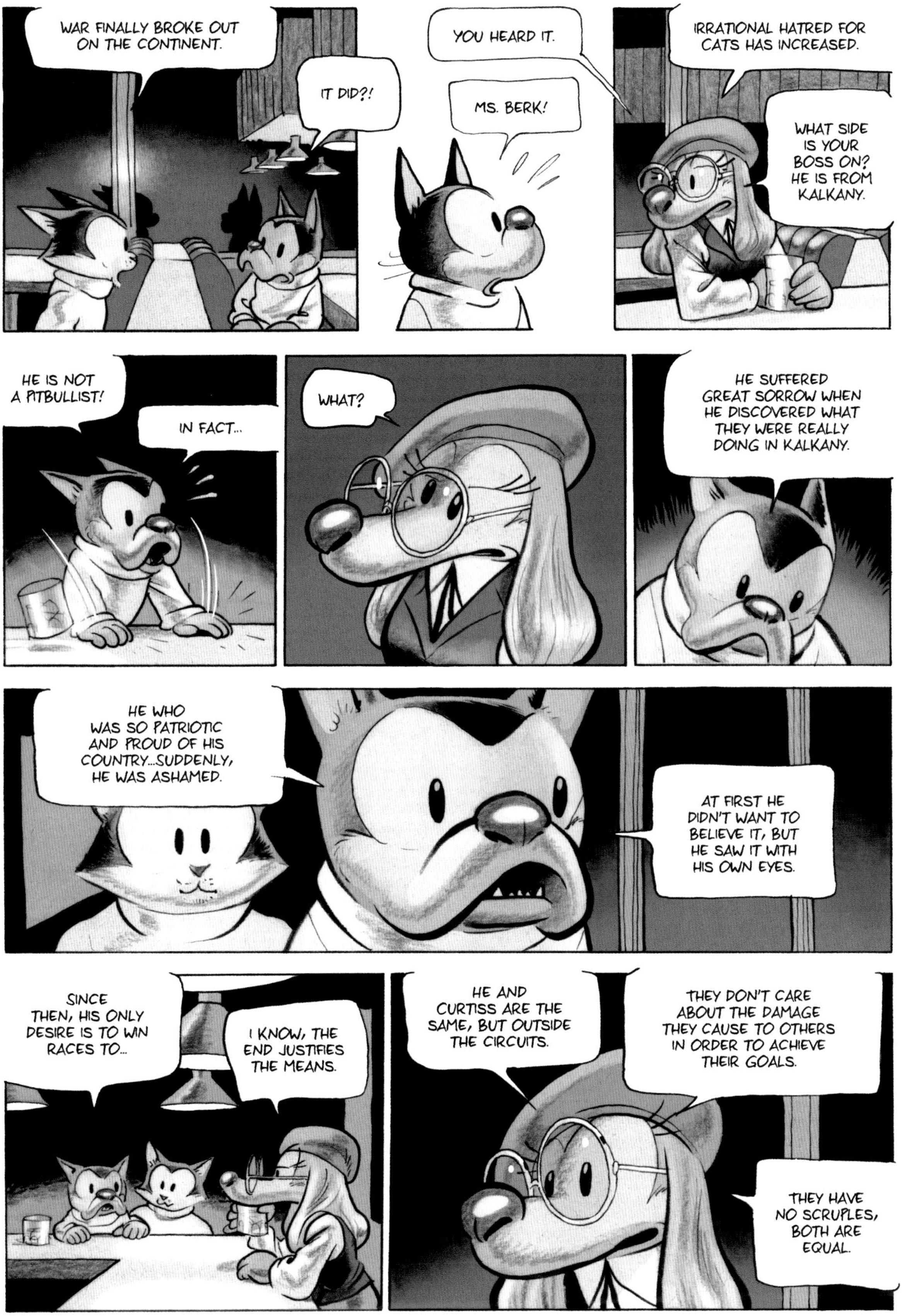
WAR FINALLY BROKE OUT ON THE CONTINENT.
IT DID?!
YOU HEARD IT.
MS. BERK!
IRRATIONAL HATRED FOR CATS HAS INCREASED.
WHAT SIDE IS YOUR BOSS ON? HE IS FROM KALKANY.
HE IS NOT A PITBULLIST!
IN FACT...
WHAT?
HE SUFFERED GREAT SORROW WHEN HE DISCOVERED WHAT THEY WERE REALLY DOING IN KALKANY.
HE WHO WAS SO PATRIOTIC AND PROUD OF HIS COUNTRY...SUDDENLY, HE WAS ASHAMED.
AT FIRST HE DIDN'T WANT TO BELIEVE IT, BUT HE SAW IT WITH HIS OWN EYES.
SINCE THEN, HIS ONLY DESIRE IS TO WIN RACES TO...
I KNOW, THE END JUSTIFIES THE MEANS.
HE AND CURTISS ARE THE SAME, BUT OUTSIDE THE CIRCUITS.
THEY DON'T CARE ABOUT THE DAMAGE THEY CAUSE TO OTHERS IN ORDER TO ACHIEVE THEIR GOALS.
THEY HAVE NO SCRUPLES, BOTH ARE EQUAL.

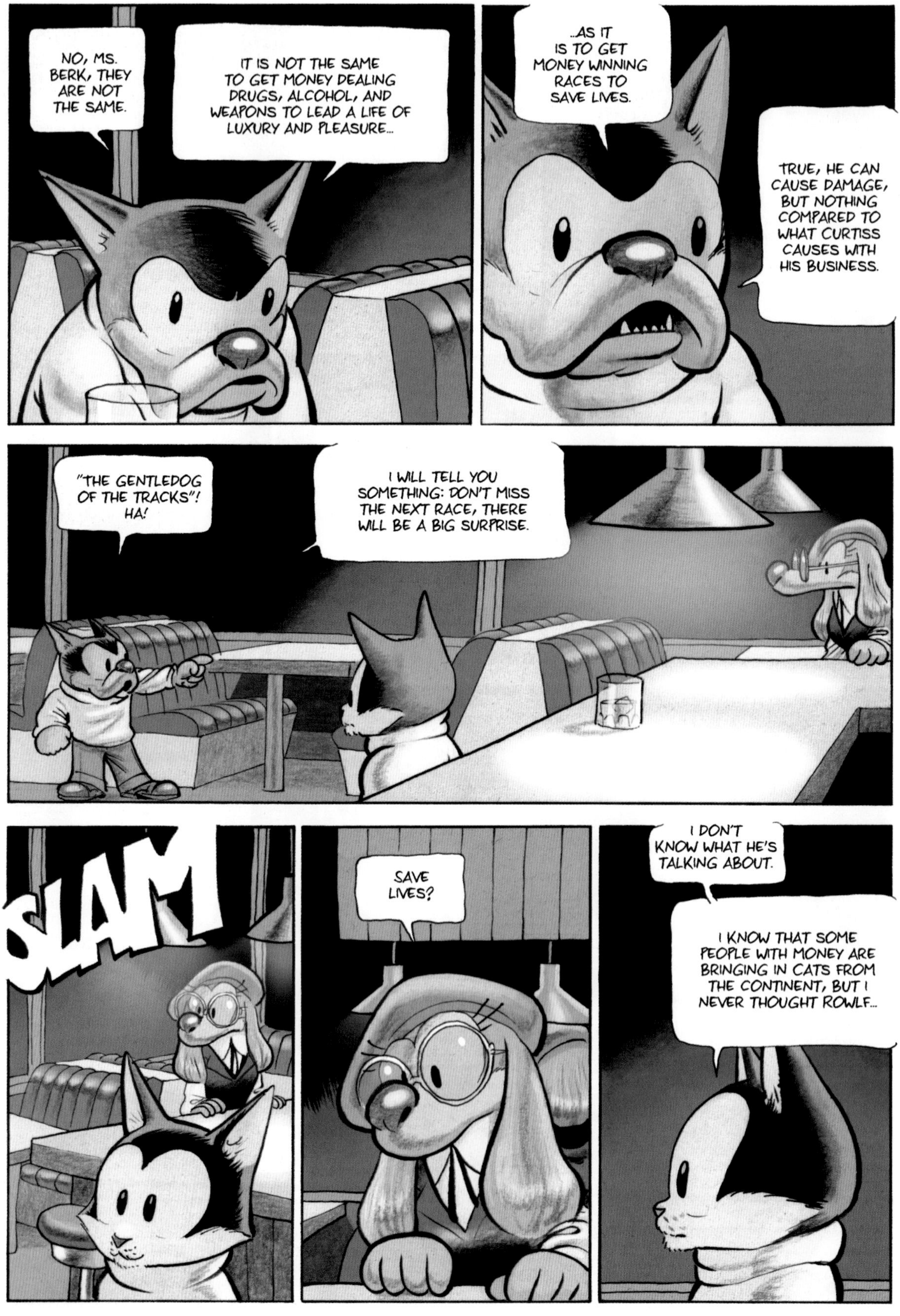
NO, MS. BERK, THEY ARE NOT THE SAME.
IT IS NOT THE SAME TO GET MONEY DEALING DRUGS, ALCOHOL, AND WEAPONS TO LEAD A LIFE OF LUXURY AND PLEASURE...
...AS IT IS TO GET MONEY WINNING RACES TO SAVE LIVES.
TRUE, HE CAN CAUSE DAMAGE, BUT NOTHING COMPARED TO WHAT CURTISS CAUSES WITH HIS BUSINESS.
"THE GENTLEDOG OF THE TRACKS"! HA!
I WILL TELL YOU SOMETHING: DON'T MISS THE NEXT RACE, THERE WILL BE A BIG SURPRISE.
SLAM
SAVE LIVES?
I DON'T KNOW WHAT HE'S TALKING ABOUT.
I KNOW THAT SOME PEOPLE WITH MONEY ARE BRINGING IN CATS FROM THE CONTINENT, BUT I NEVER THOUGHT ROWLF...

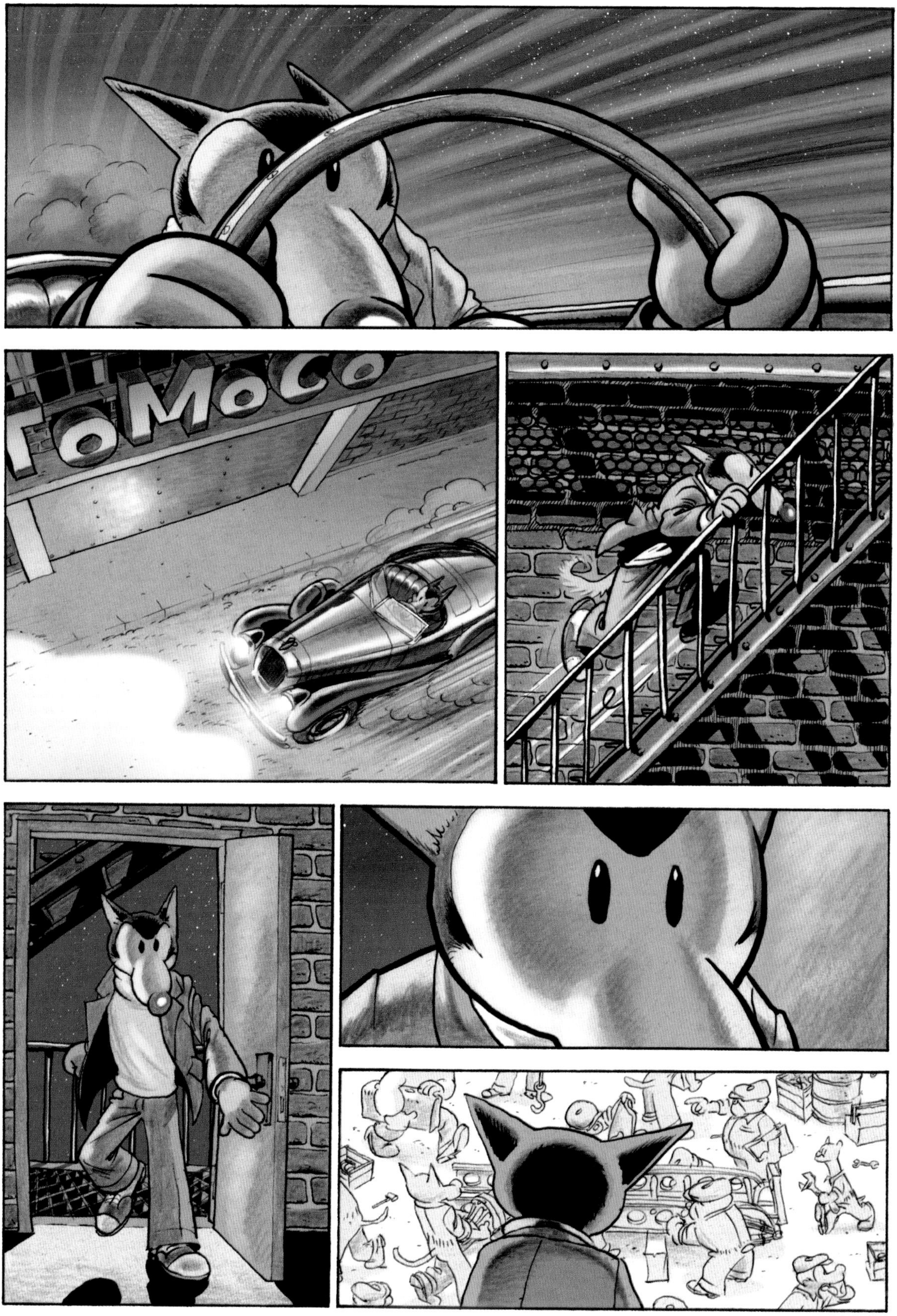
ToMoCo

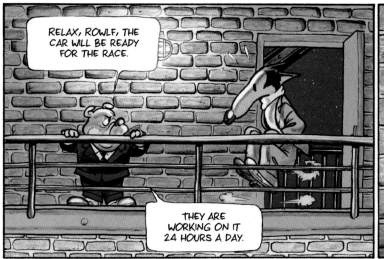

RELAX, ROWLF, THE CAR WILL BE READY FOR THE RACE.

THEY ARE WORKING ON IT 24 HOURS A DAY.

WHAT WILL DINO SAY WHEN HE SEES IT?

HE WON'T SAY ANYTHING. WE HAVE GONE TO THE PATENT OFFICE AND REGISTERED HIS DESIGNS. HE DIDN'T DO IT.

IT'S NOT HIS CAR ANYMORE, ROWLF. IT'S TOMOCO'S.

HA! HA! HA!

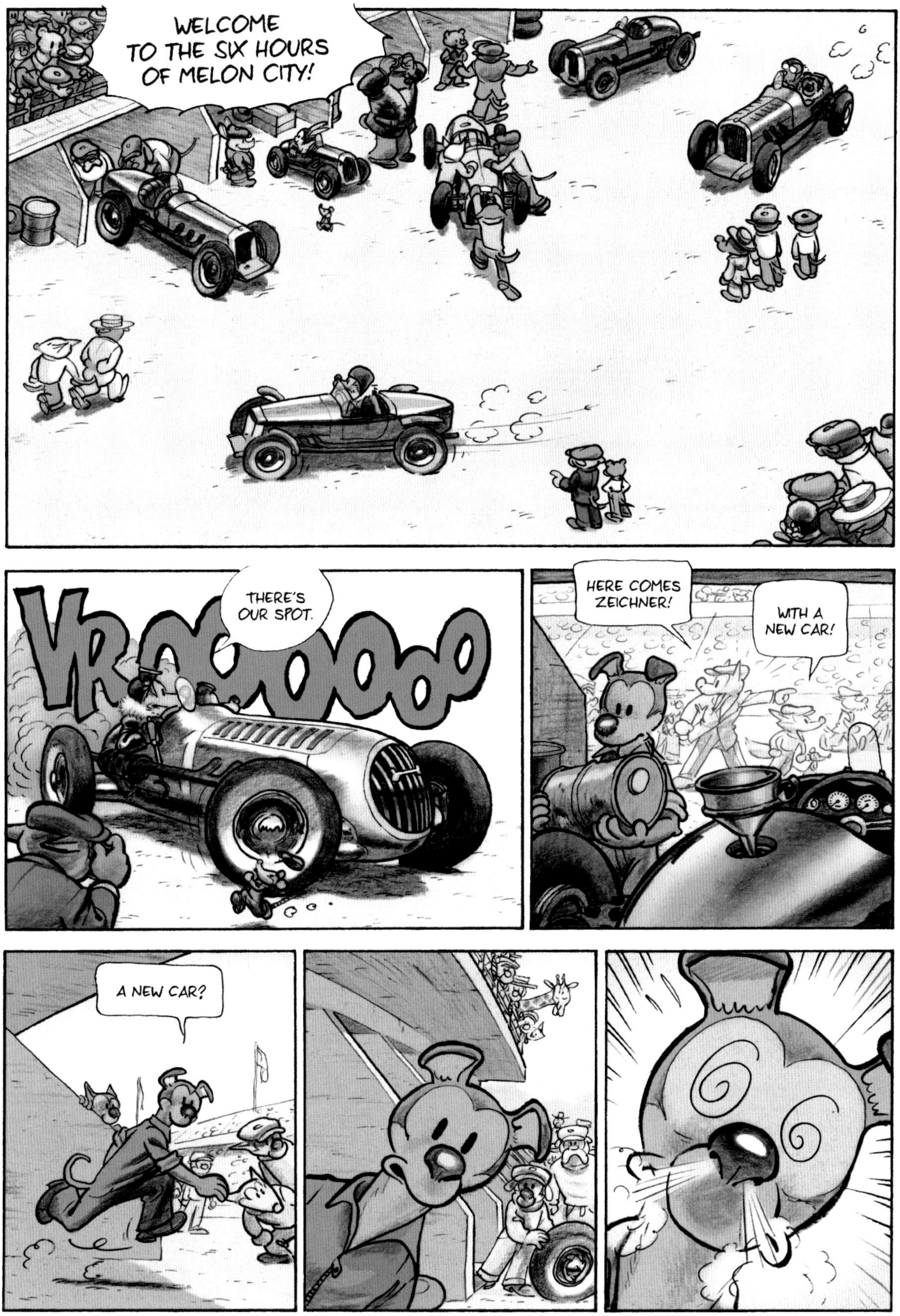
WELCOME TO THE SIX HOURS OF MELON CITY!
VROOOOOOO
THERE'S OUR SPOT.
HERE COMES ZEICHNER!
WITH A NEW CAR!
A NEW CAR?

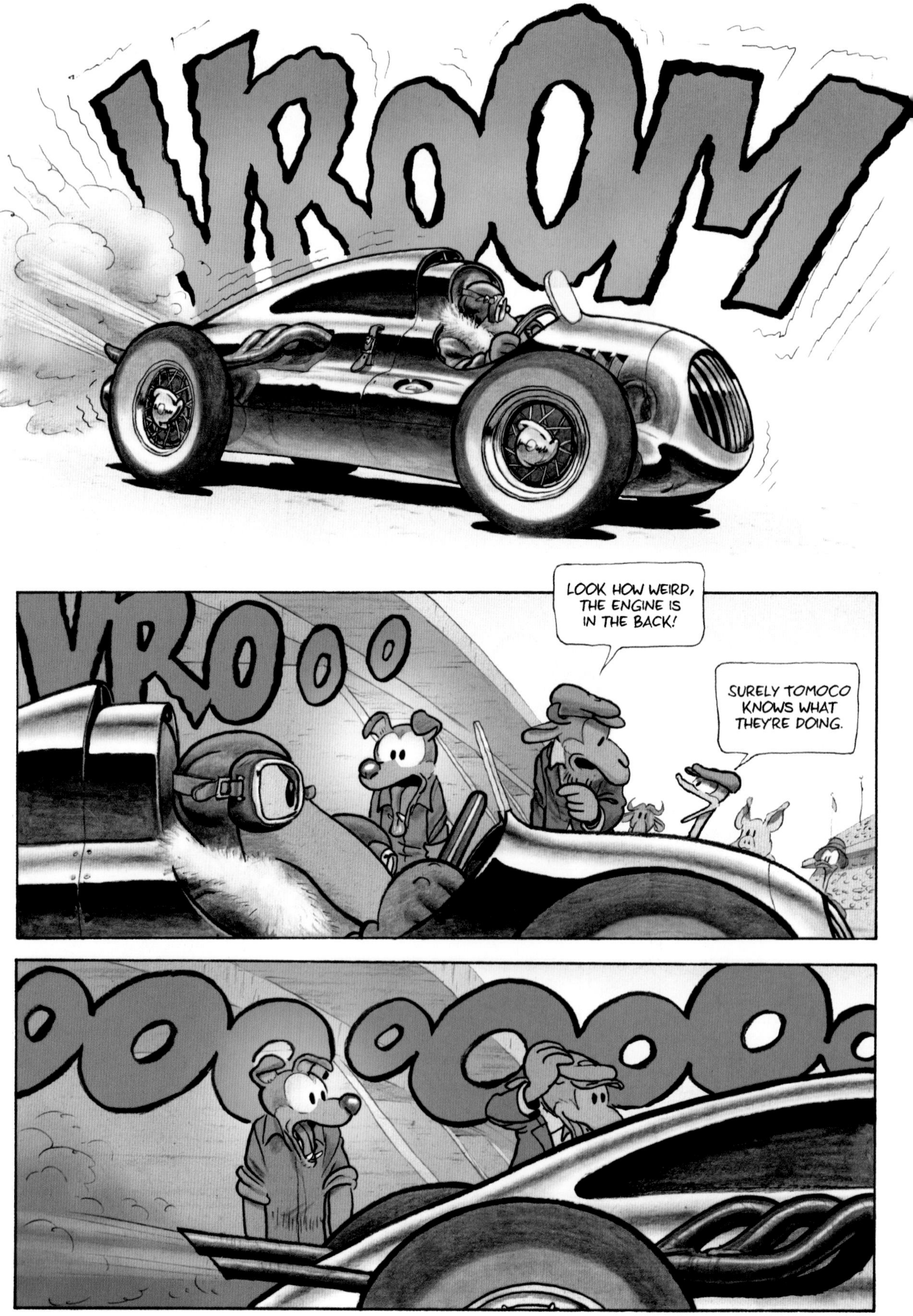
VROOM
VROOO
LOOK HOW WEIRD, THE ENGINE IS IN THE BACK!
SURELY TOMOCO KNOWS WHAT THEY'RE DOING.
OOOOOOOO

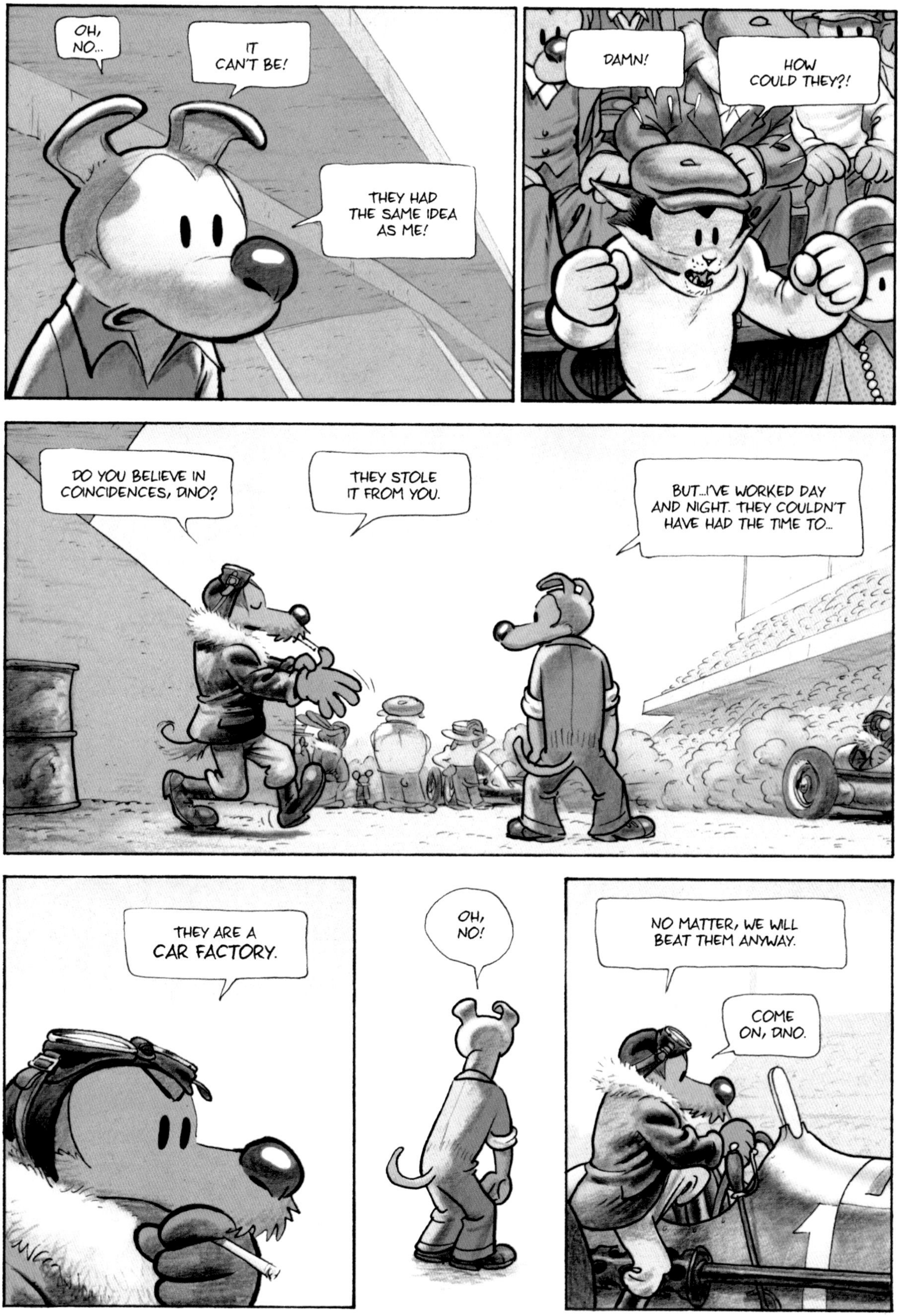
OH, NO...
IT CAN'T BE!
THEY HAD THE SAME IDEA AS ME!
DAMN!
HOW COULD THEY?!
DO YOU BELIEVE IN COINCIDENCES, DINO?
THEY STOLE IT FROM YOU.
BUT...I'VE WORKED DAY AND NIGHT. THEY COULDN'T HAVE HAD THE TIME TO...
THEY ARE A CAR FACTORY.
OH, NO!
NO MATTER, WE WILL BEAT THEM ANYWAY.
COME ON, DINO.

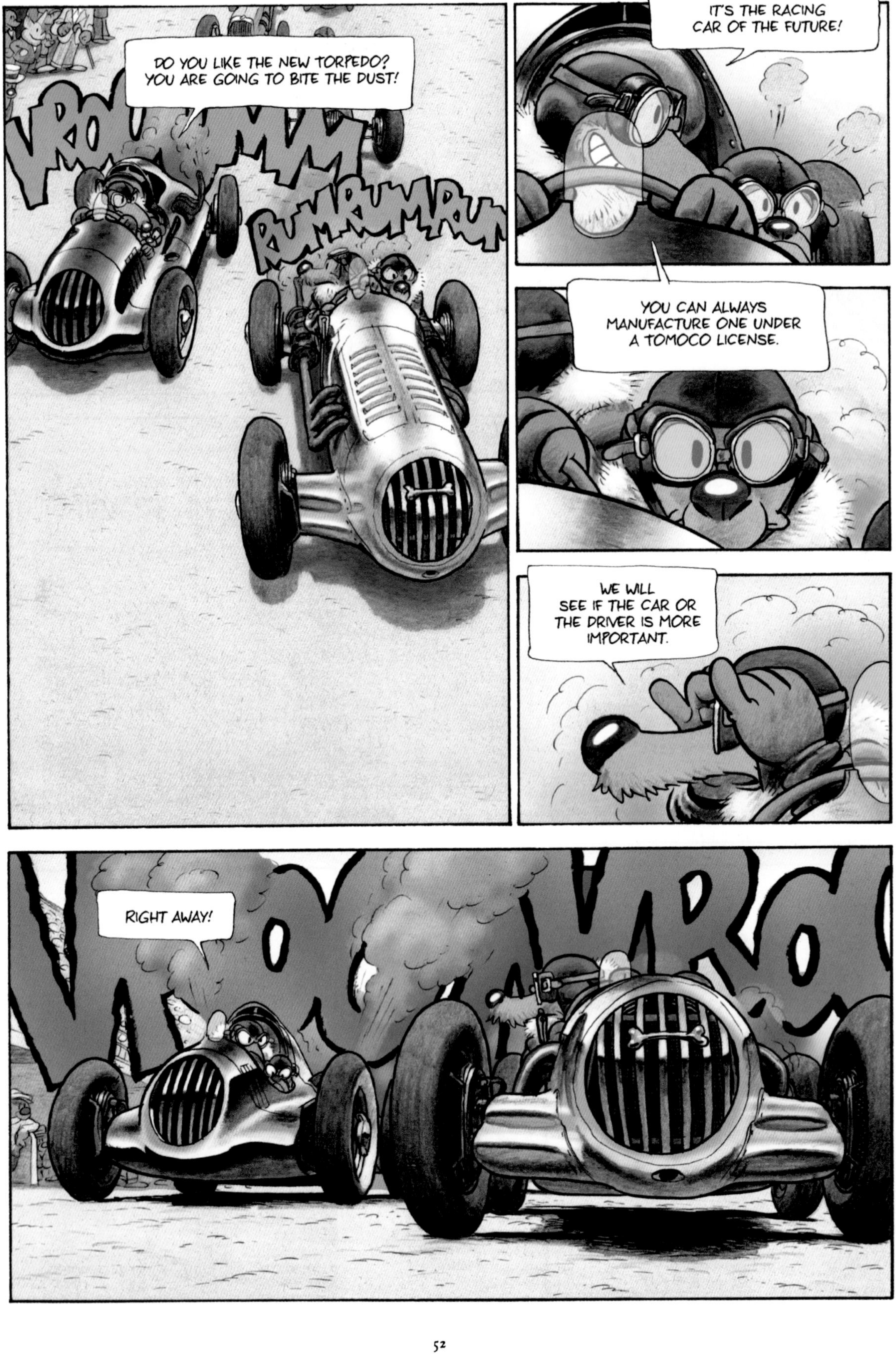
DO YOU LIKE THE NEW TORPEDO? YOU ARE GOING TO BITE THE DUST!
IT'S THE RACING CAR OF THE FUTURE!
YOU CAN ALWAYS MANUFACTURE ONE UNDER A TOMOCO LICENSE.
WE WILL SEE IF THE CAR OR THE DRIVER IS MORE IMPORTANT.
RIGHT AWAY!

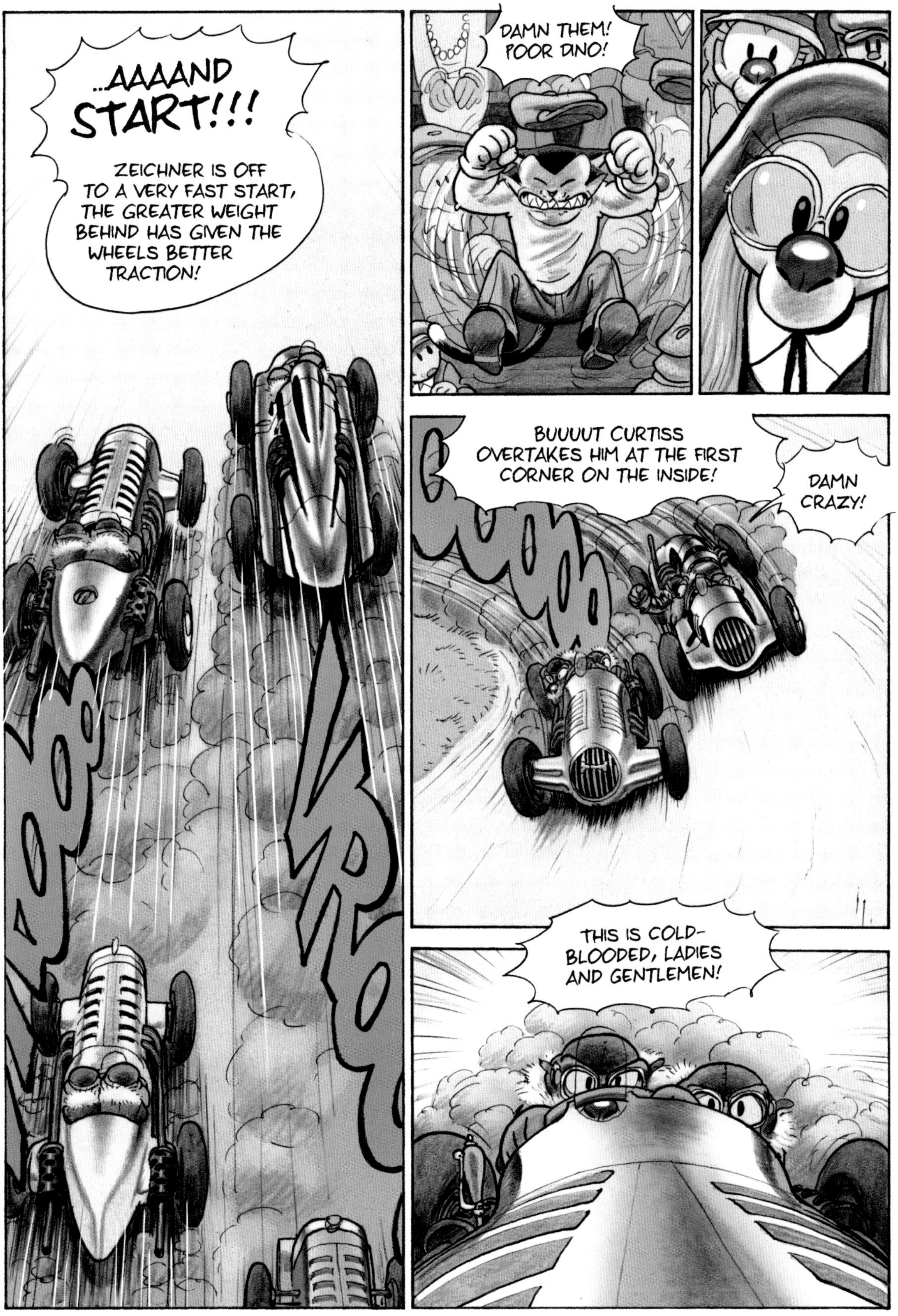
..AAAAND START!!!
ZEICHNER IS OFF TO A VERY FAST START, THE GREATER WEIGHT BEHIND HAS GIVEN THE WHEELS BETTER TRACTION!
DAMN THEM! POOR DINO!
BUUUUT CURTISS OVERTAKES HIM AT THE FIRST CORNER ON THE INSIDE!
DAMN CRAZY!
THIS IS COLD-BLOODED, LADIES AND GENTLEMEN!

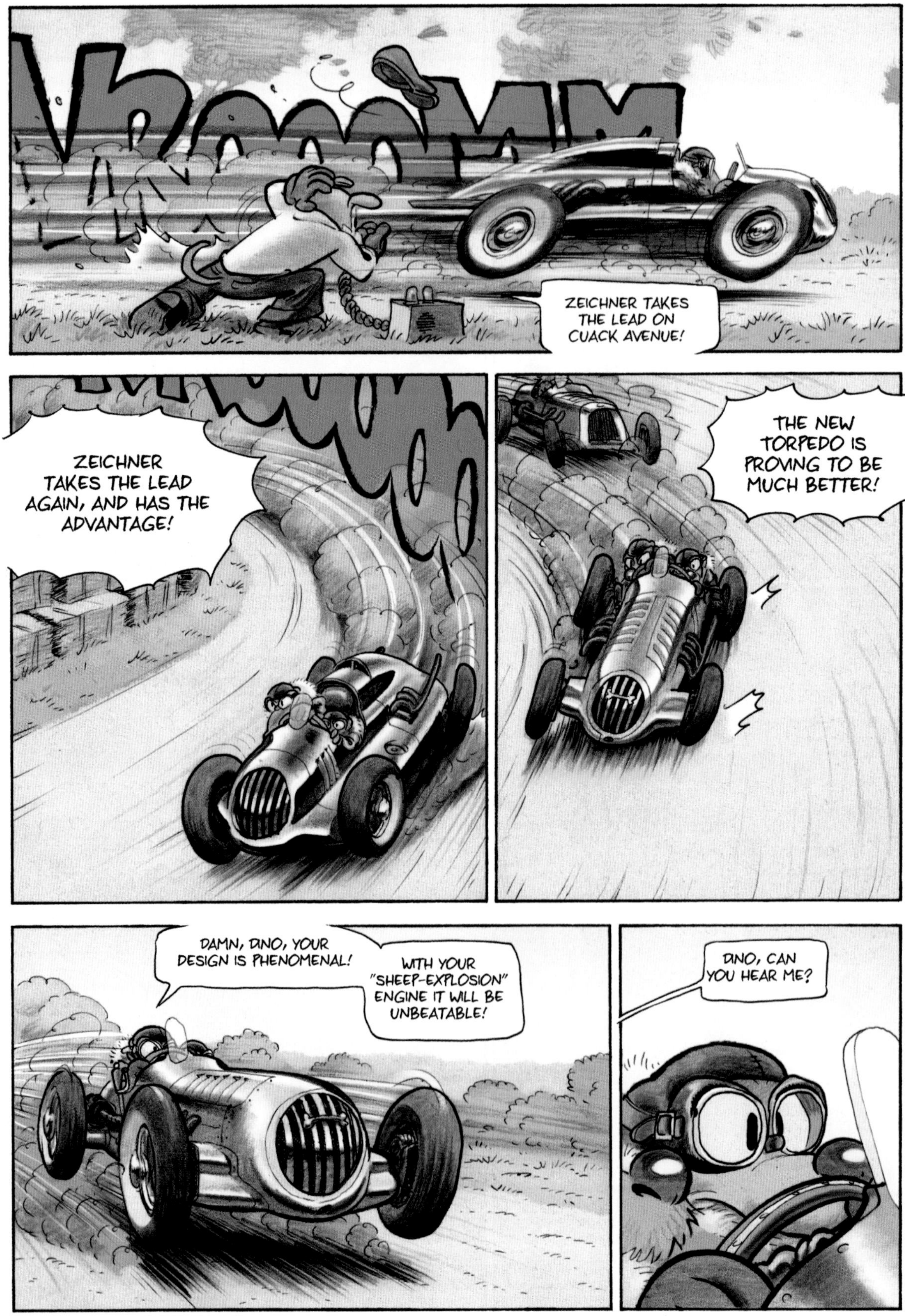
VROOOMM
ZEICHNER TAKES THE LEAD ON CUACK AVENUE!
ZEICHNER TAKES THE LEAD AGAIN, AND HAS THE ADVANTAGE!
THE NEW TORPEDO IS PROVING TO BE MUCH BETTER!
DAMN, DINO, YOUR DESIGN IS PHENOMENAL!
WITH YOUR "SHEEP-EXPLOSION" ENGINE IT WILL BE UNBEATABLE!
DINO, CAN YOU HEAR ME?

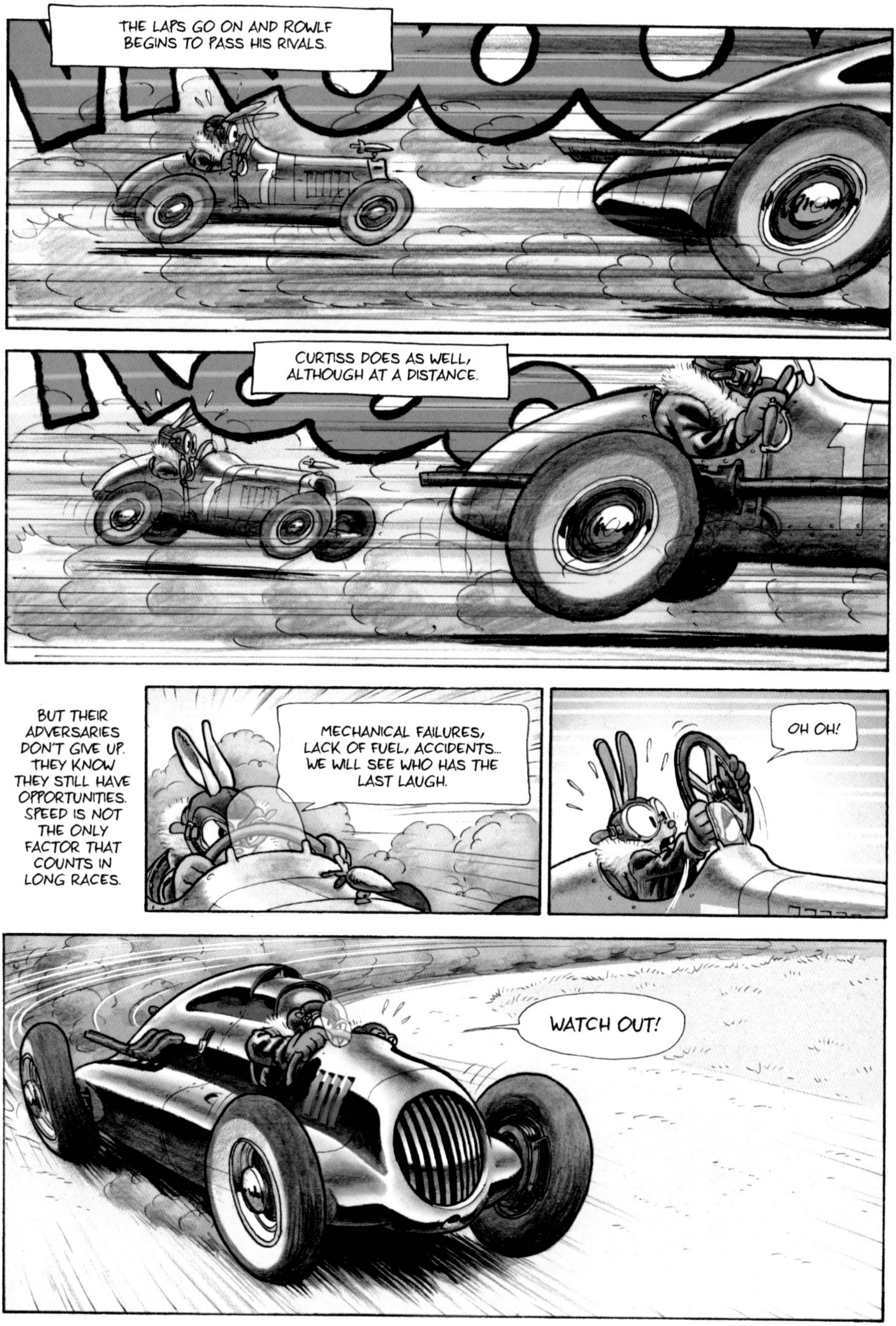
THE LAPS GO ON AND ROWLF BEGINS TO PASS HIS RIVALS.
CURTISS DOES AS WELL, ALTHOUGH AT A DISTANCE.
BUT THEIR ADVERSARIES DON'T GIVE UP. THEY KNOW THEY STILL HAVE OPPORTUNITIES. SPEED IS NOT THE ONLY FACTOR THAT COUNTS IN LONG RACES.
MECHANICAL FAILURES, LACK OF FUEL, ACCIDENTS... WE WILL SEE WHO HAS THE LAST LAUGH.
OH OH!
WATCH OUT!

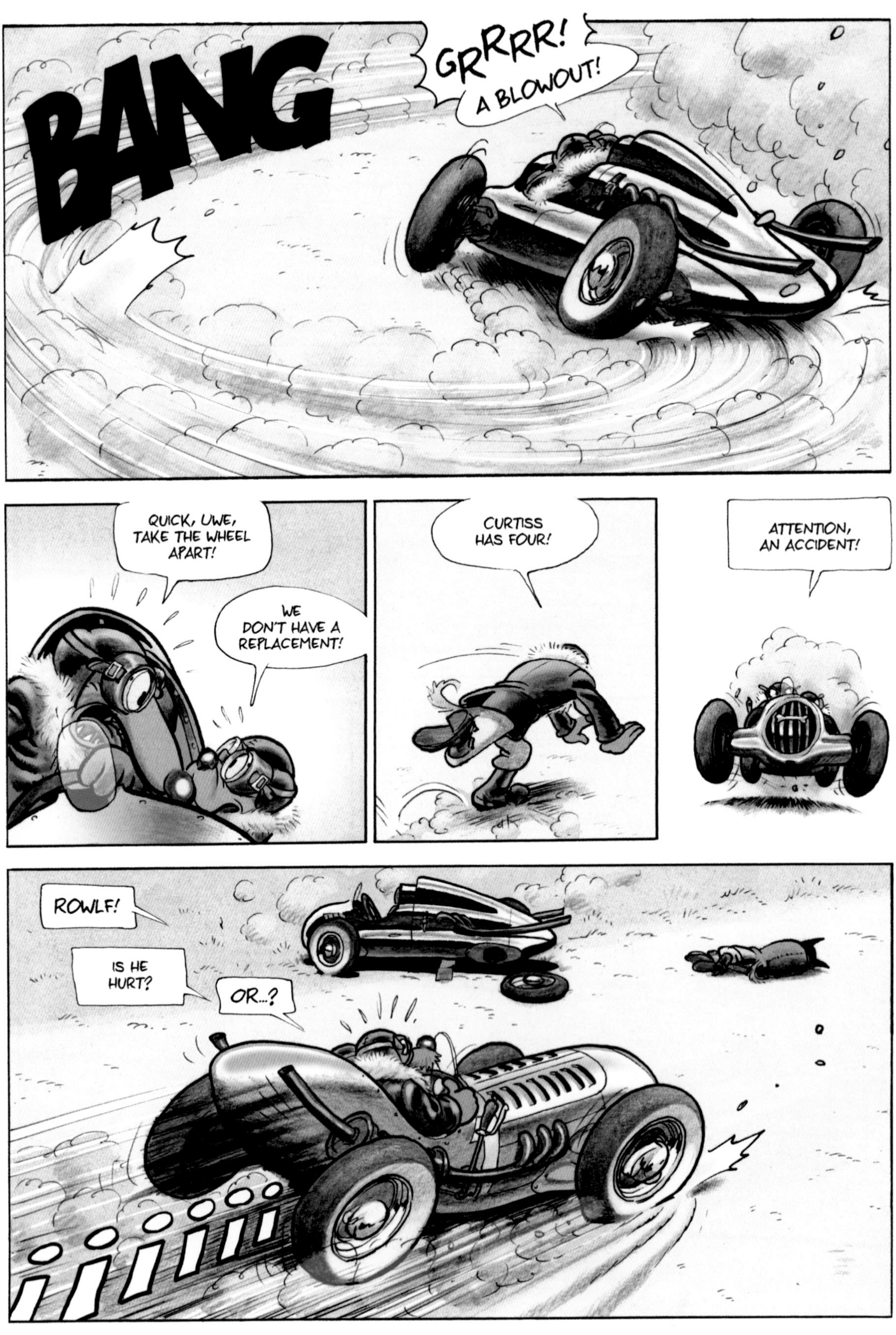
BANG
GRRRR!
A BLOWOUT!
QUICK, UWE, TAKE THE WHEEL APART!
WE DON'T HAVE A REPLACEMENT!
CURTISS HAS FOUR!
ATTENTION, AN ACCIDENT!
ROWLF!
IS HE HURT?
OR...?

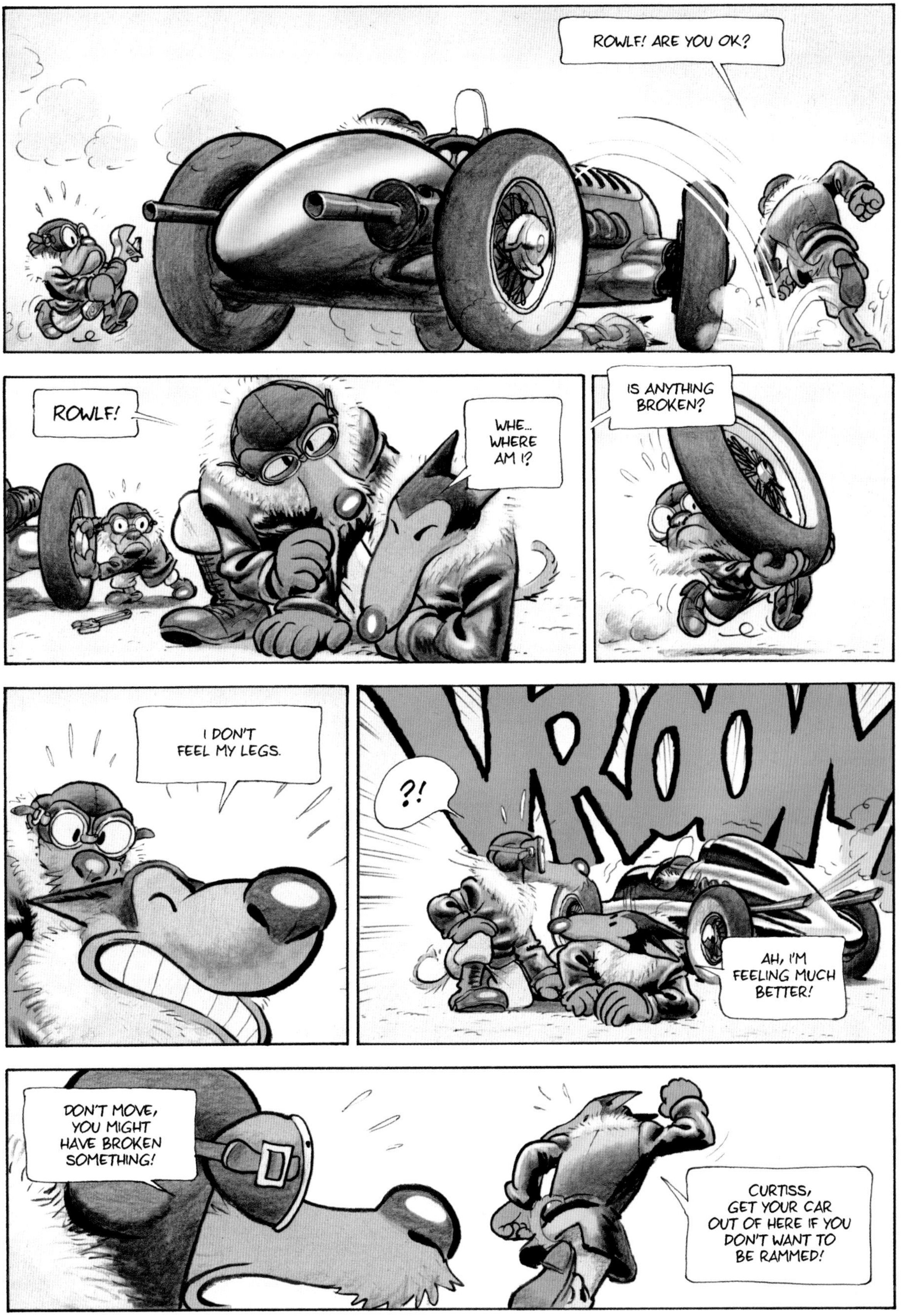

ROWLF! ARE YOU OK?
ROWLF!
WHE... WHERE AM I?
IS ANYTHING BROKEN?
I DON'T FEEL MY LEGS.
VROOM
?!
AH, I'M FEELING MUCH BETTER!
DON'T MOVE, YOU MIGHT HAVE BROKEN SOMETHING!
CURTISS, GET YOUR CAR OUT OF HERE IF YOU DON'T WANT TO BE RAMMED!

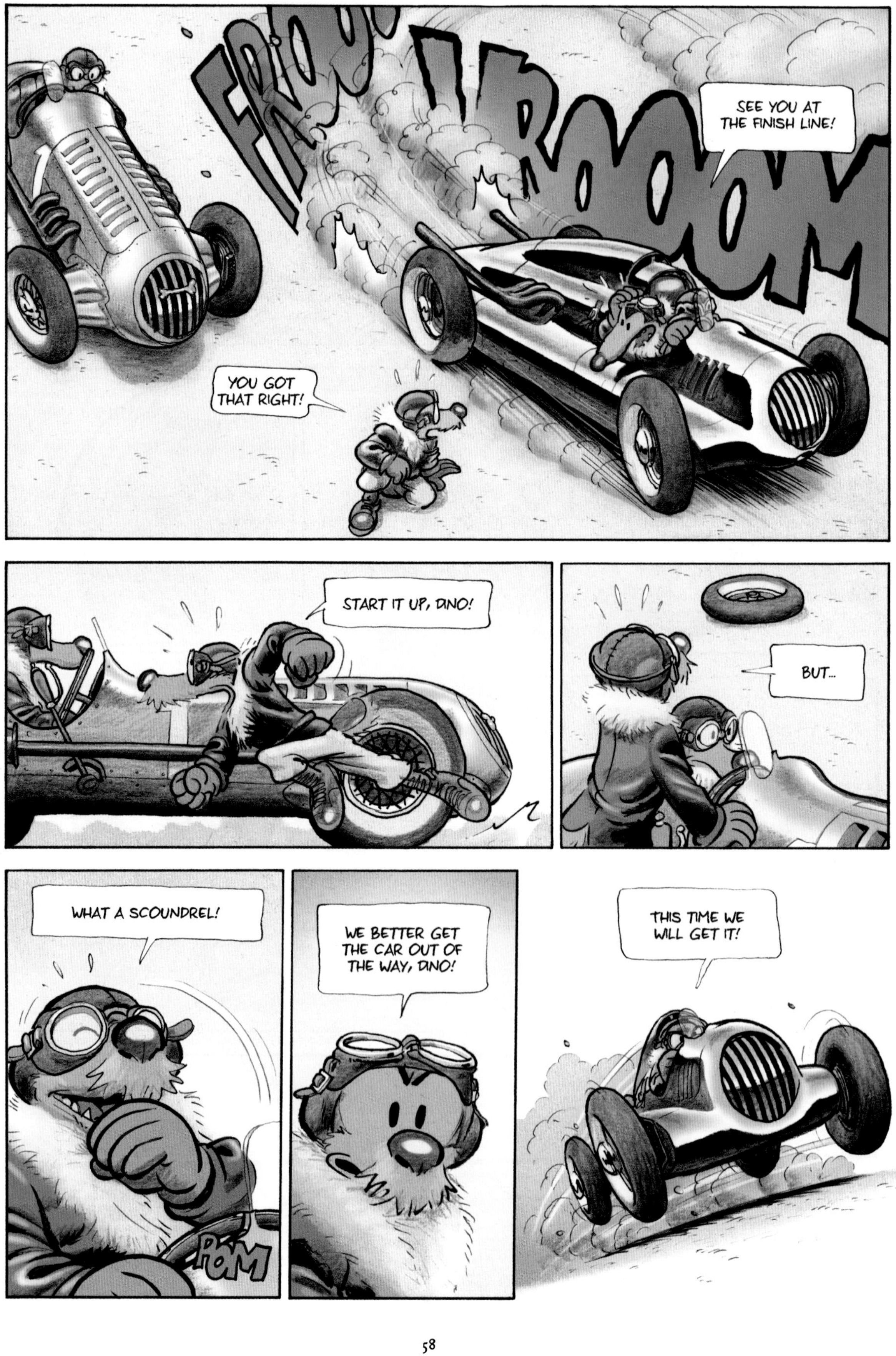
VROOOOM
SEE YOU AT THE FINISH LINE!
YOU GOT THAT RIGHT!
START IT UP, DINO!
BUT...
WHAT A SCOUNDREL!
POM
WE BETTER GET THE CAR OUT OF THE WAY, DINO!
THIS TIME WE WILL GET IT!

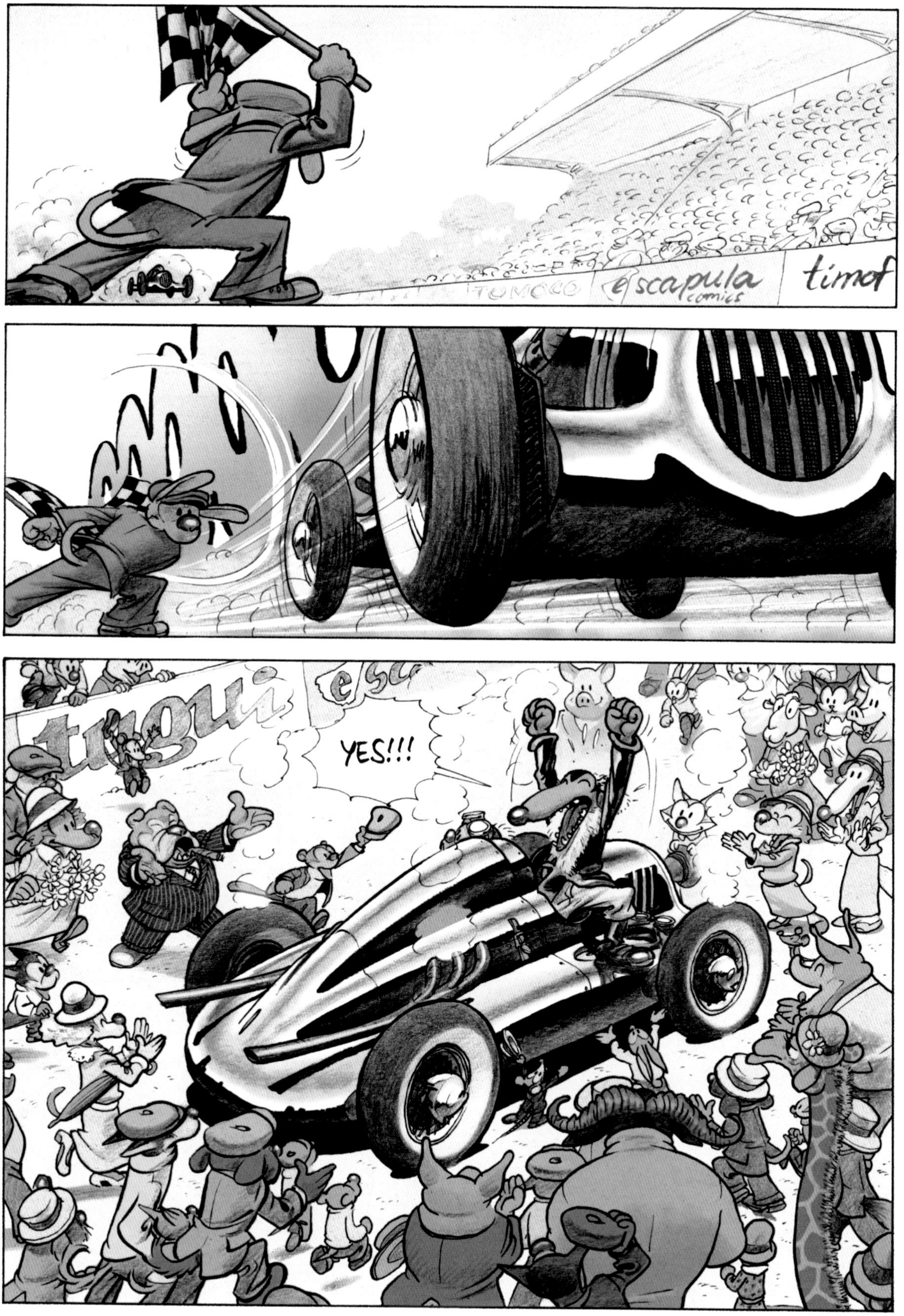
TOMOCO
e/scapula comics
timof
YES!!!

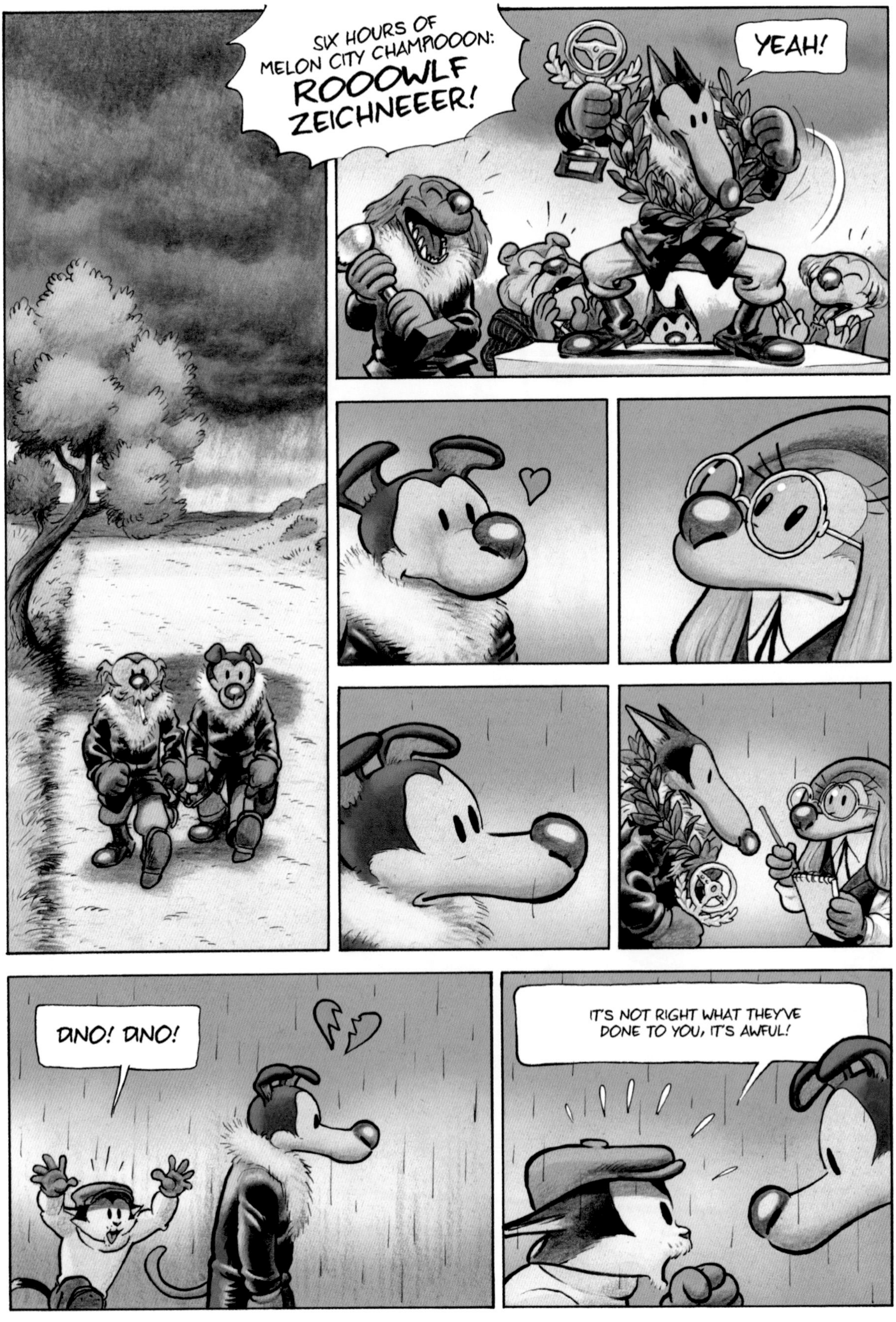
SIX HOURS OF MELON CITY CHAMPIOOON: ROOOWLF ZEICHNEEER!
YEAH!
DINO! DINO!
IT'S NOT RIGHT WHAT THEY'VE DONE TO YOU, IT'S AWFUL!

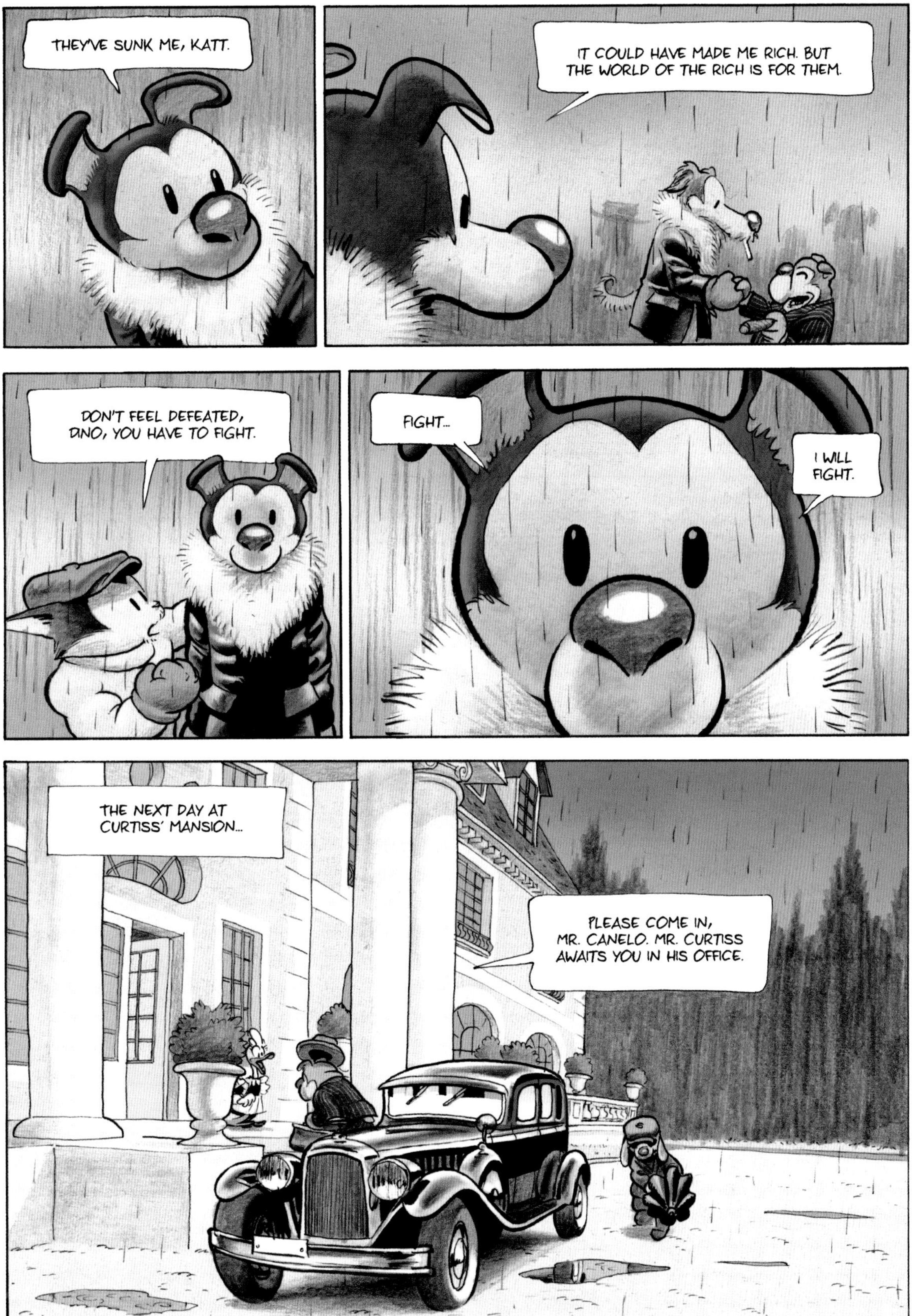
THEY'VE SUNK ME, KATT.
IT COULD HAVE MADE ME RICH. BUT THE WORLD OF THE RICH IS FOR THEM.
DON'T FEEL DEFEATED, DINO, YOU HAVE TO FIGHT.
FIGHT...
I WILL FIGHT.
THE NEXT DAY AT CURTISS' MANSION...
PLEASE COME IN, MR. CANELO. MR. CURTISS AWAITS YOU IN HIS OFFICE.

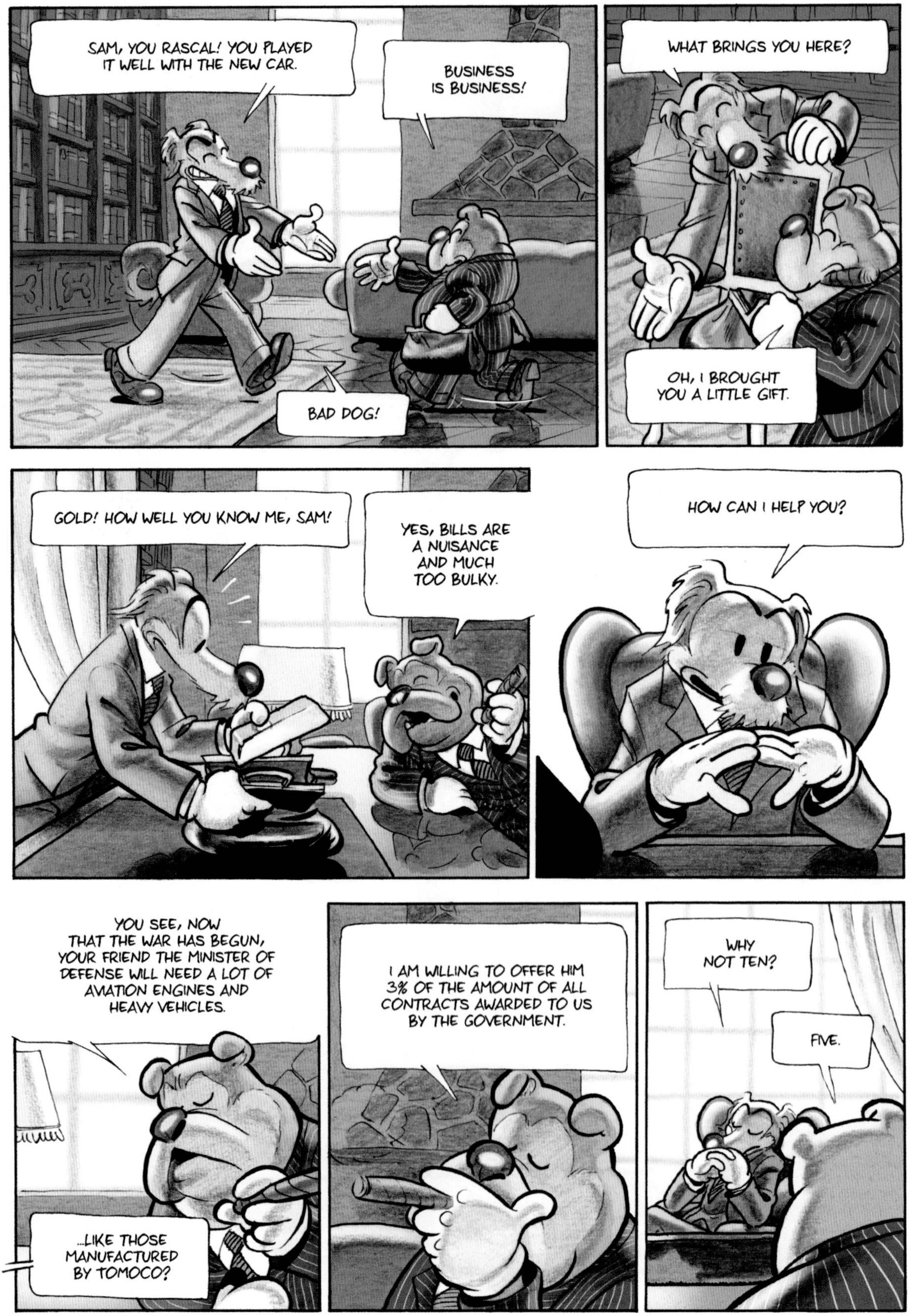
SAM, YOU RASCAL! YOU PLAYED IT WELL WITH THE NEW CAR.
BUSINESS IS BUSINESS!
BAD DOG!
WHAT BRINGS YOU HERE?
OH, I BROUGHT YOU A LITTLE GIFT.
GOLD! HOW WELL YOU KNOW ME, SAM!
YES, BILLS ARE A NUISANCE AND MUCH TOO BULKY.
HOW CAN I HELP YOU?
YOU SEE, NOW THAT THE WAR HAS BEGUN, YOUR FRIEND THE MINISTER OF DEFENSE WILL NEED A LOT OF AVIATION ENGINES AND HEAVY VEHICLES.
...LIKE THOSE MANUFACTURED BY TOMOCO?
I AM WILLING TO OFFER HIM 3% OF THE AMOUNT OF ALL CONTRACTS AWARDED TO US BY THE GOVERNMENT.
WHY NOT TEN?
FIVE.

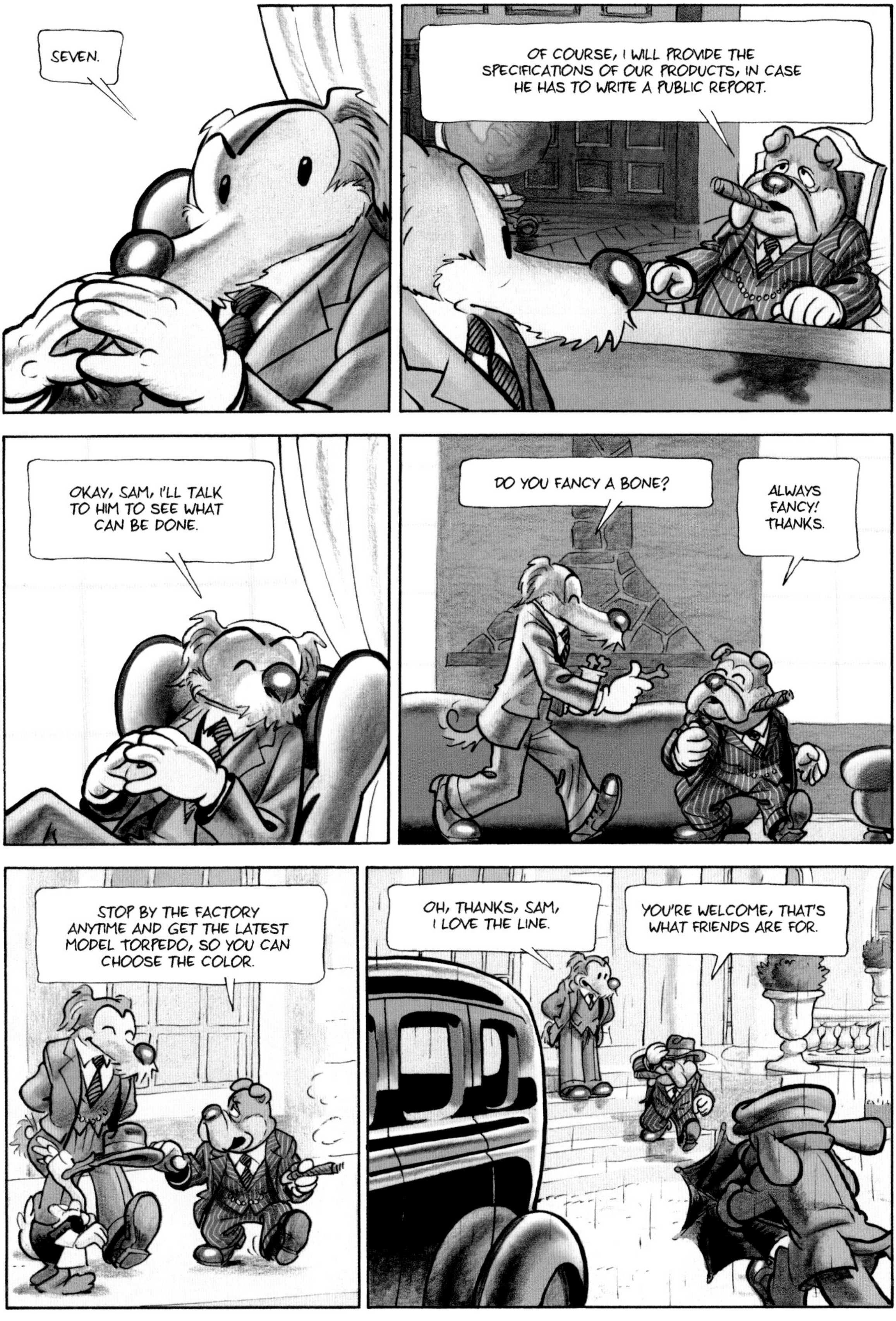
SEVEN.
OF COURSE, I WILL PROVIDE THE SPECIFICATIONS OF OUR PRODUCTS, IN CASE HE HAS TO WRITE A PUBLIC REPORT.
OKAY, SAM, I'LL TALK TO HIM TO SEE WHAT CAN BE DONE.
DO YOU FANCY A BONE?
ALWAYS FANCY! THANKS.
STOP BY THE FACTORY ANYTIME AND GET THE LATEST MODEL TORPEDO, SO YOU CAN CHOOSE THE COLOR.
OH, THANKS, SAM, I LOVE THE LINE.
YOU'RE WELCOME, THAT'S WHAT FRIENDS ARE FOR.

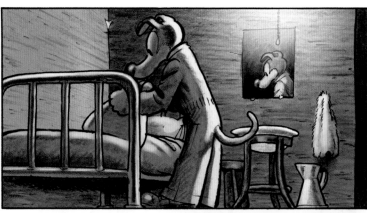

FIGHT...

I'LL FIGHT.

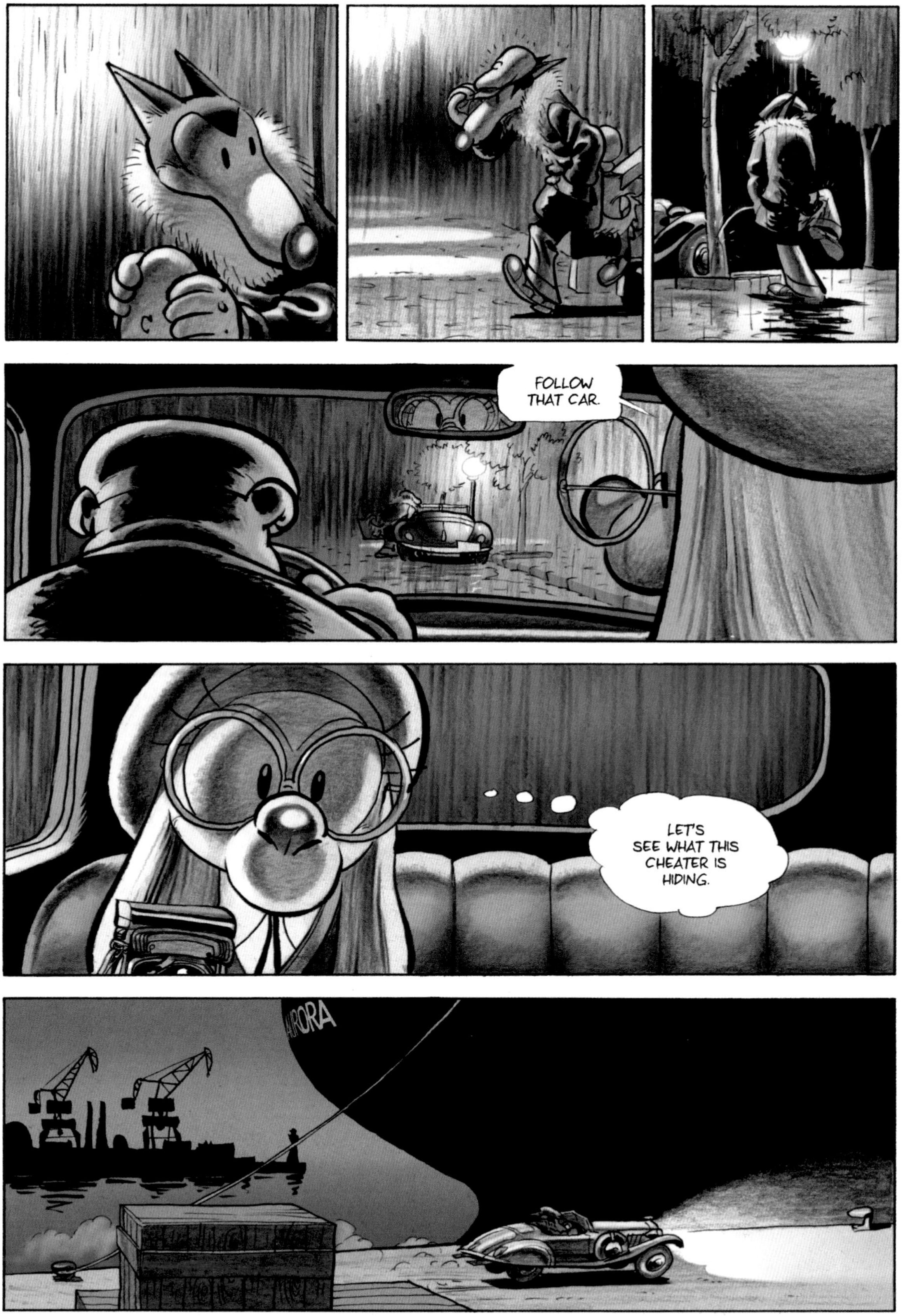
FOLLOW THAT CAR.
LET'S SEE WHAT THIS CHEATER IS HIDING.
AURORA

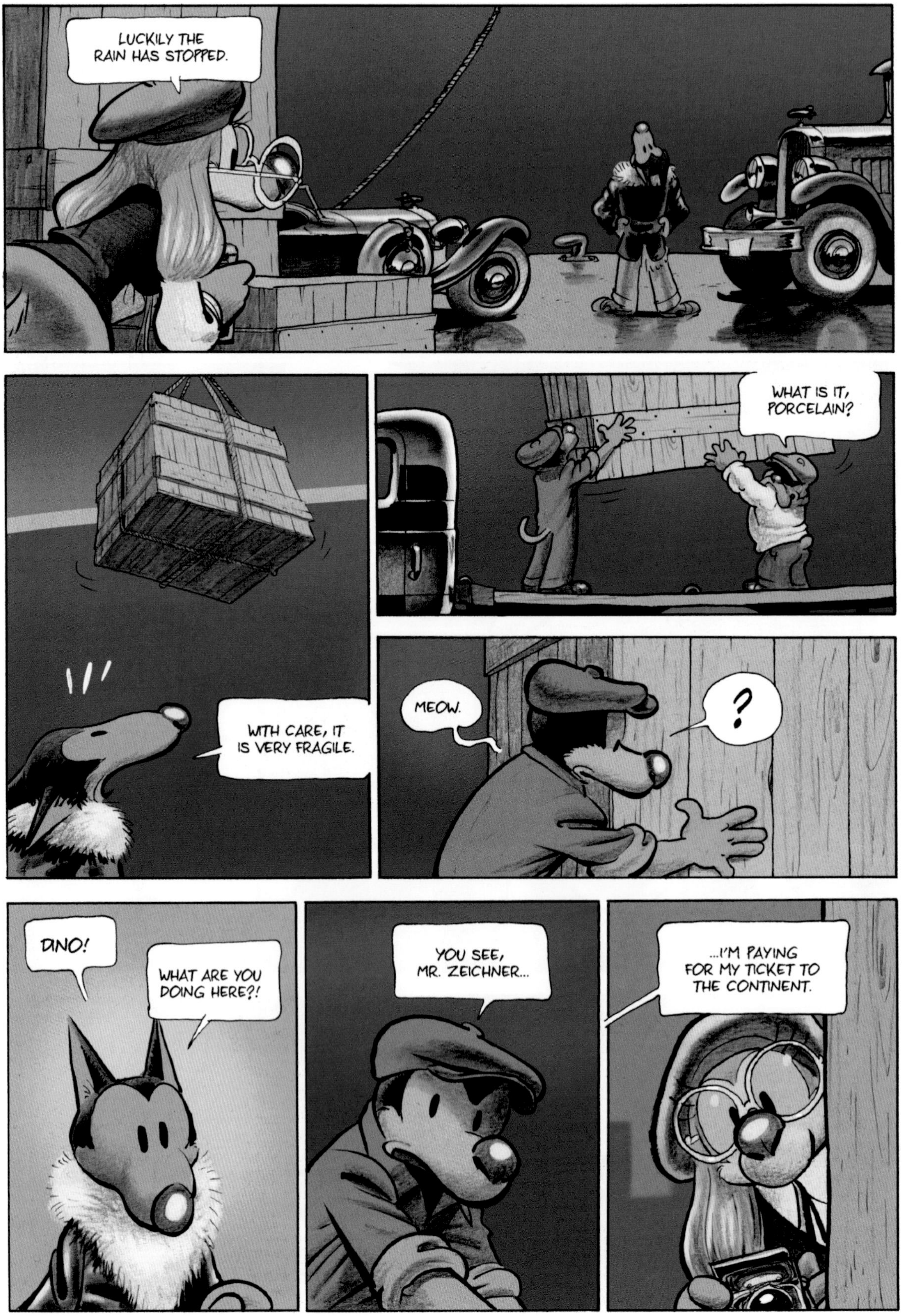
LUCKILY THE RAIN HAS STOPPED.
WHAT IS IT, PORCELAIN?
WITH CARE, IT IS VERY FRAGILE.
MEOW.
?
DINO!
WHAT ARE YOU DOING HERE?!
YOU SEE, MR. ZEICHNER...
...I'M PAYING FOR MY TICKET TO THE CONTINENT.

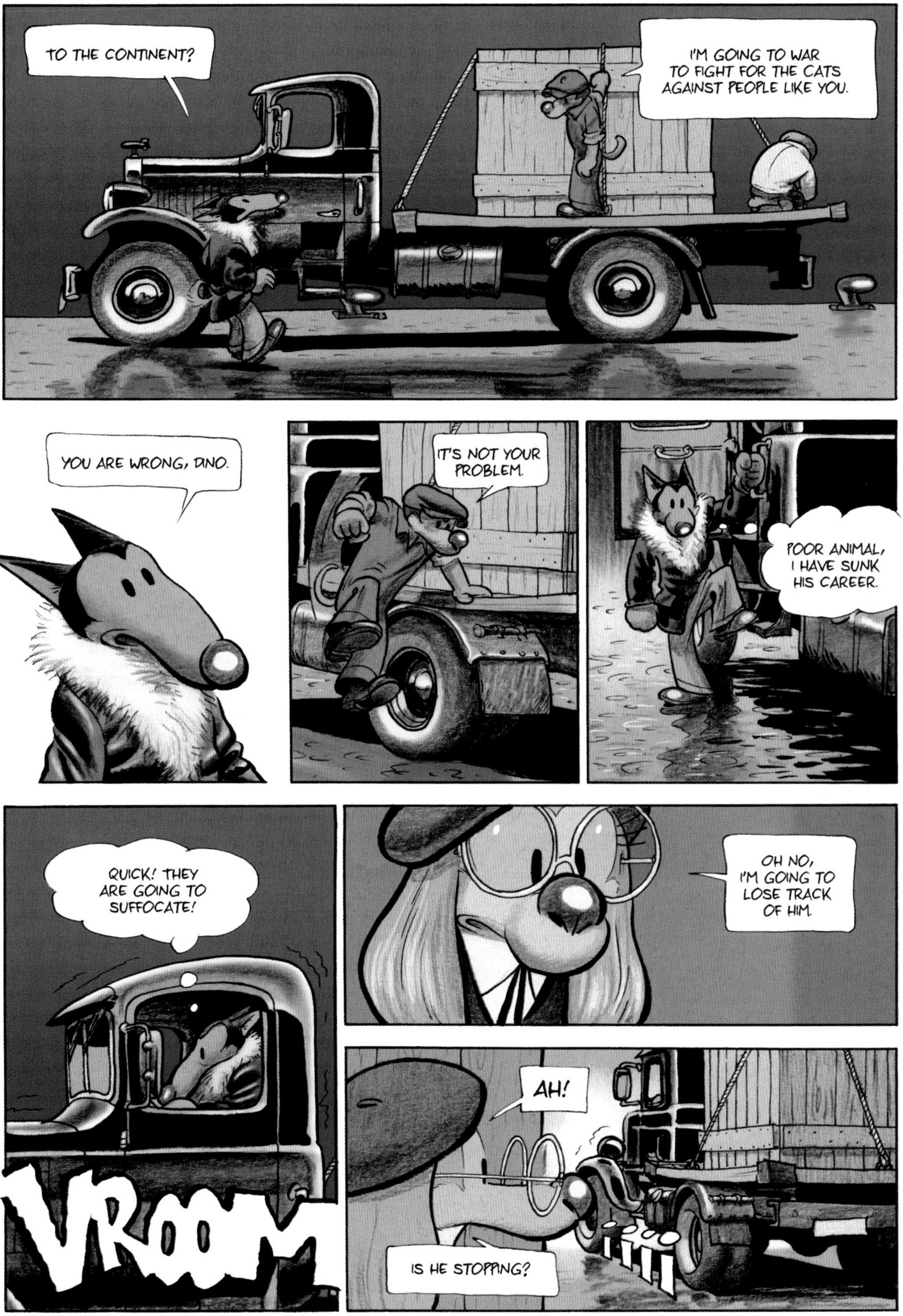
TO THE CONTINENT?
I'M GOING TO WAR TO FIGHT FOR THE CATS AGAINST PEOPLE LIKE YOU.
YOU ARE WRONG, DINO.
IT'S NOT YOUR PROBLEM.
POOR ANIMAL, I HAVE SUNK HIS CAREER.
QUICK! THEY ARE GOING TO SUFFOCATE!
VROOM
OH NO, I'M GOING TO LOSE TRACK OF HIM.
AH!
IS HE STOPPING?

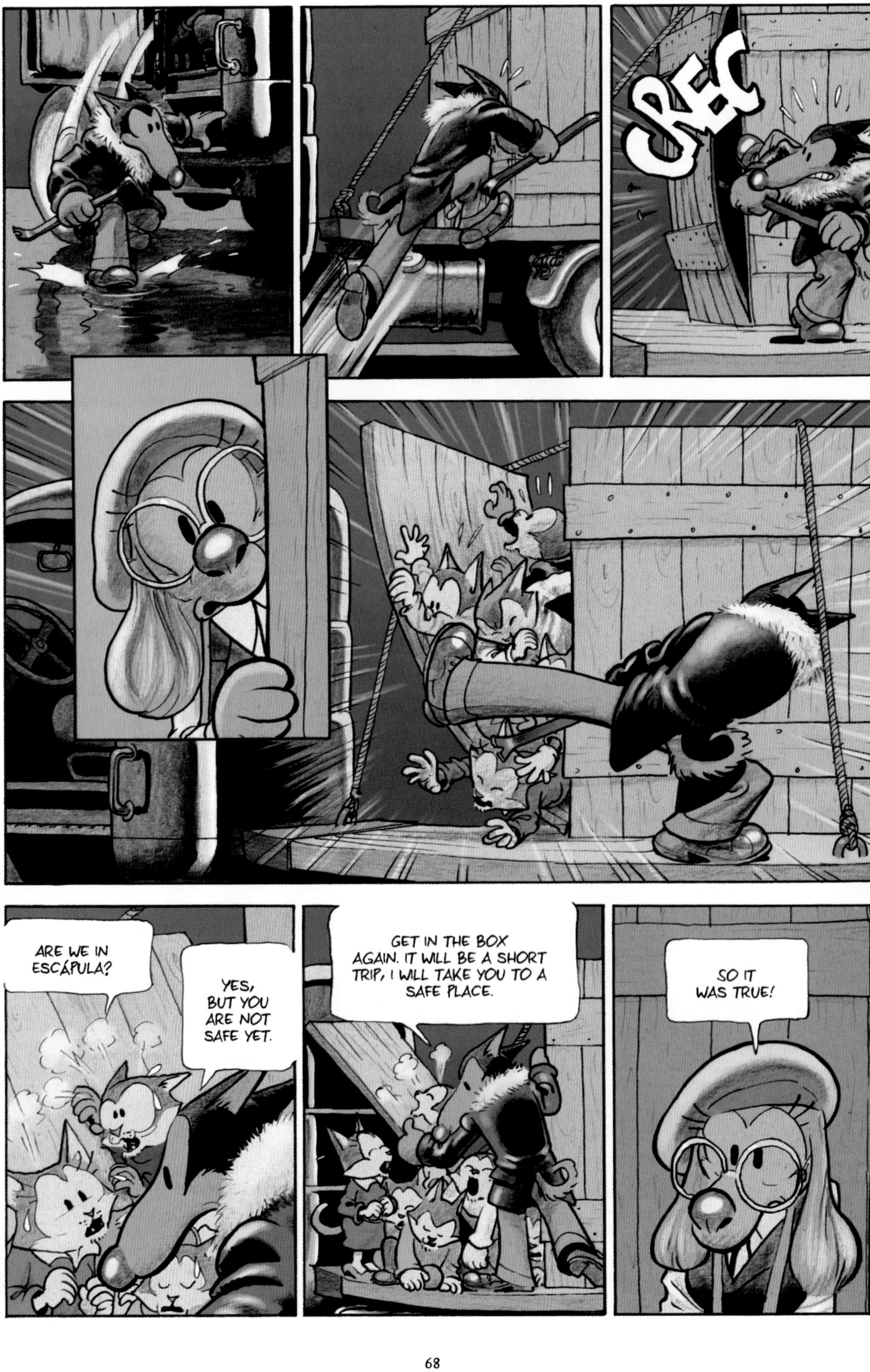
CREC
ARE WE IN ESCÁPULA?
YES, BUT YOU ARE NOT SAFE YET.
GET IN THE BOX AGAIN. IT WILL BE A SHORT TRIP, I WILL TAKE YOU TO A SAFE PLACE.
SO IT WAS TRUE!

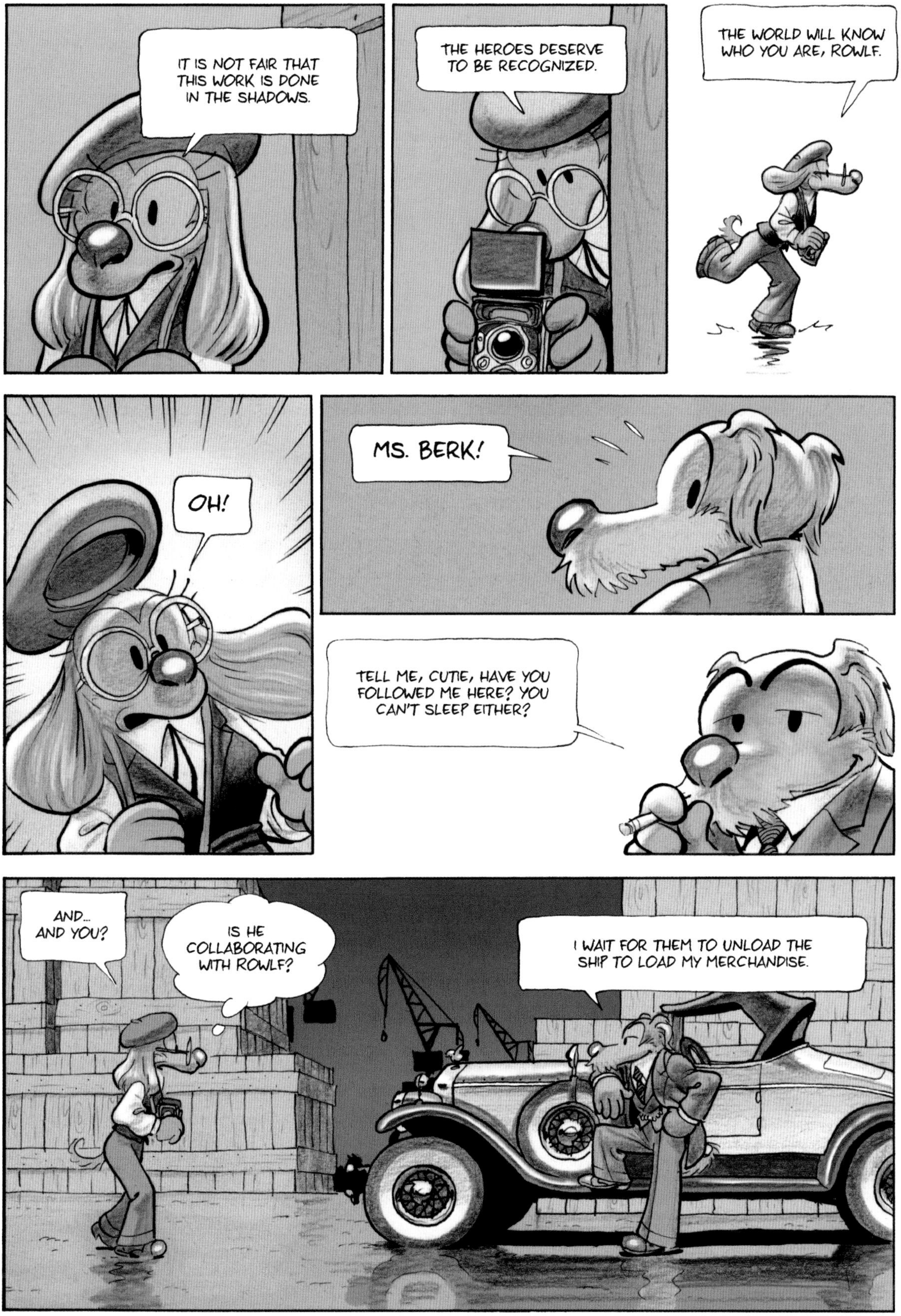
IT IS NOT FAIR THAT THIS WORK IS DONE IN THE SHADOWS.
THE HEROES DESERVE TO BE RECOGNIZED.
THE WORLD WILL KNOW WHO YOU ARE, ROWLF.
OH!
MS. BERK!
TELL ME, CUTIE, HAVE YOU FOLLOWED ME HERE? YOU CAN'T SLEEP EITHER?
AND... AND YOU?
IS HE COLLABORATING WITH ROWLF?
I WAIT FOR THEM TO UNLOAD THE SHIP TO LOAD MY MERCHANDISE.

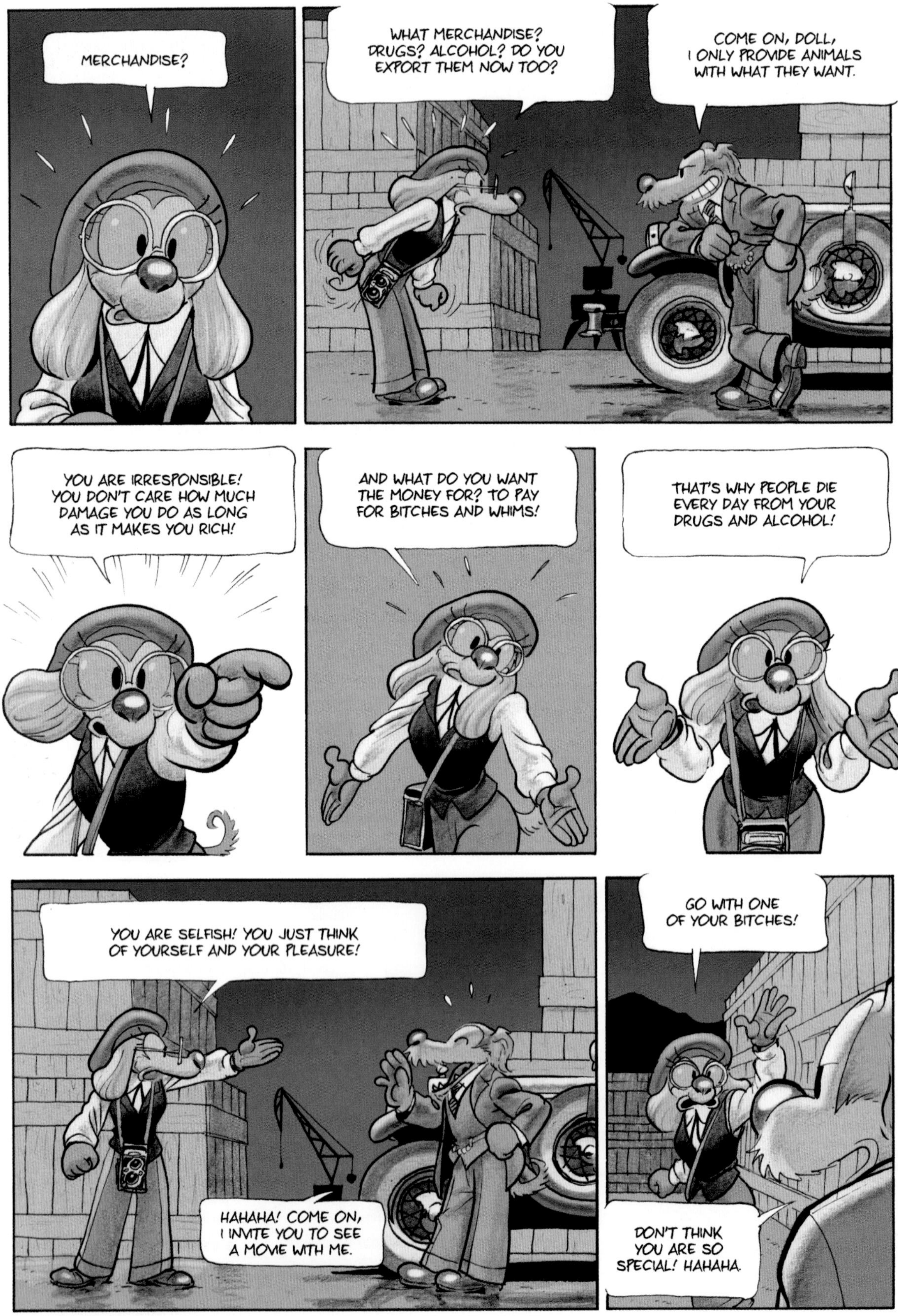
MERCHANDISE?
WHAT MERCHANDISE? DRUGS? ALCOHOL? DO YOU EXPORT THEM NOW TOO?
COME ON, DOLL, I ONLY PROVIDE ANIMALS WITH WHAT THEY WANT.
YOU ARE IRRESPONSIBLE! YOU DON'T CARE HOW MUCH DAMAGE YOU DO AS LONG AS IT MAKES YOU RICH!
AND WHAT DO YOU WANT THE MONEY FOR? TO PAY FOR BITCHES AND WHIMS!
THAT'S WHY PEOPLE DIE EVERY DAY FROM YOUR DRUGS AND ALCOHOL!
YOU ARE SELFISH! YOU JUST THINK OF YOURSELF AND YOUR PLEASURE!
HAHAHA! COME ON, I INVITE YOU TO SEE A MOVIE WITH ME.
GO WITH ONE OF YOUR BITCHES!
DON'T THINK YOU ARE SO SPECIAL! HAHAHA.

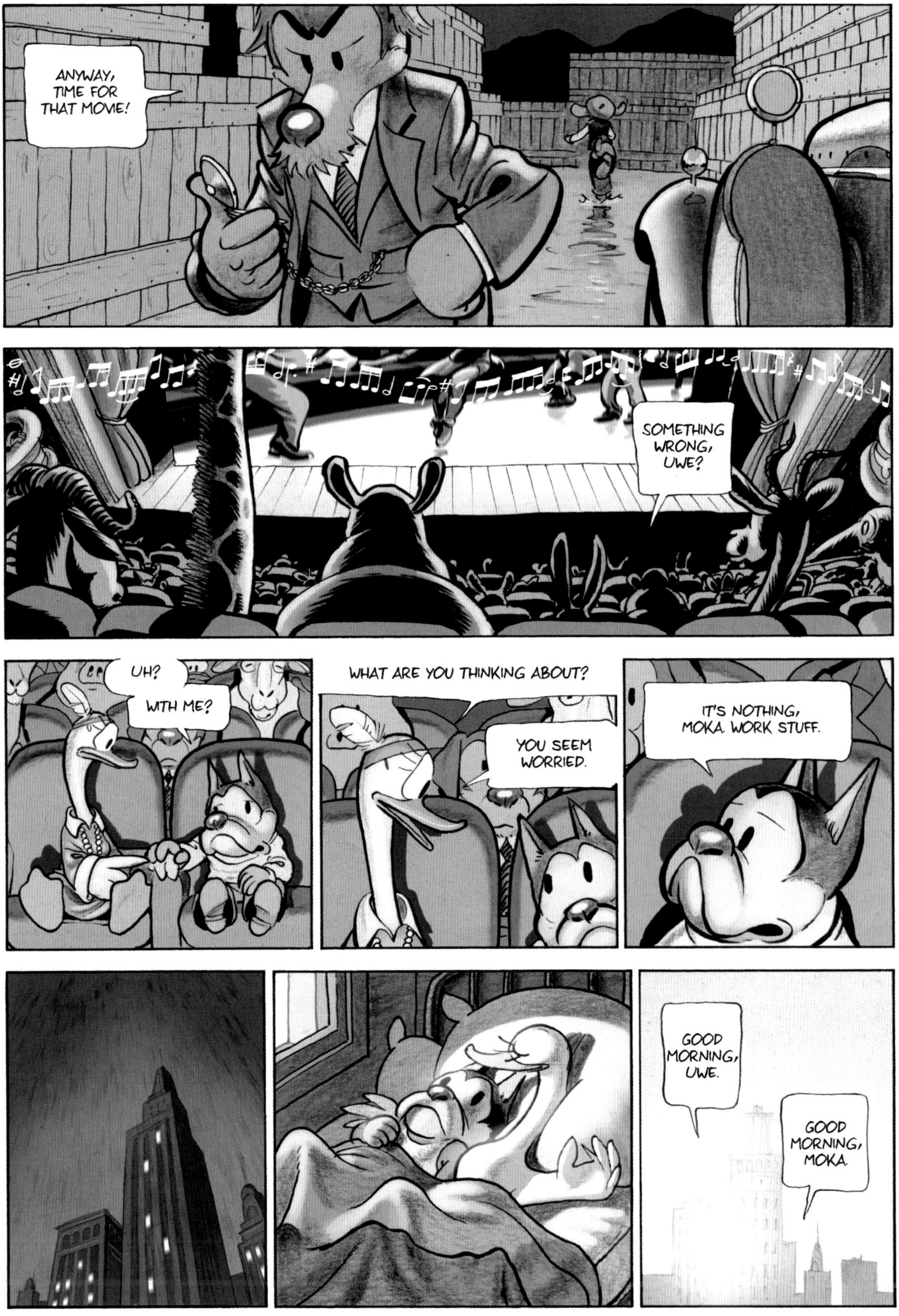
ANYWAY, TIME FOR THAT MOVIE!
SOMETHING WRONG, UWE?
UH?
WITH ME?
WHAT ARE YOU THINKING ABOUT?
YOU SEEM WORRIED.
IT'S NOTHING, MOKA. WORK STUFF.
GOOD MORNING, UWE.
GOOD MORNING, MOKA.

YOU GOT UP SO EARLY!

I HAVEN'T SLEPT ALL NIGHT.

WHAT'S WRONG?

DINO HAS GONE TO WAR.

WHAT?! OUR DINO?!

YES.

AND IT'S MY FAULT.

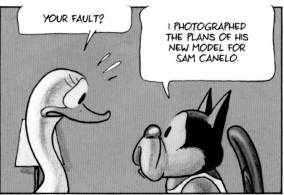

YOUR FAULT?

I PHOTOGRAPHED THE PLANS OF HIS NEW MODEL FOR SAM CANELO.

I HAVE TO TELL MR. CURTISS RIGHT AWAY! HE WILL BE ABLE TO DO SOMETHING!

HOW DID HE GO?

ON A CARGO BOAT THAT LEFT PIER 3 LAST NIGHT OFF THE WEST DOCK.

LATER ON...

DINO...WHY?

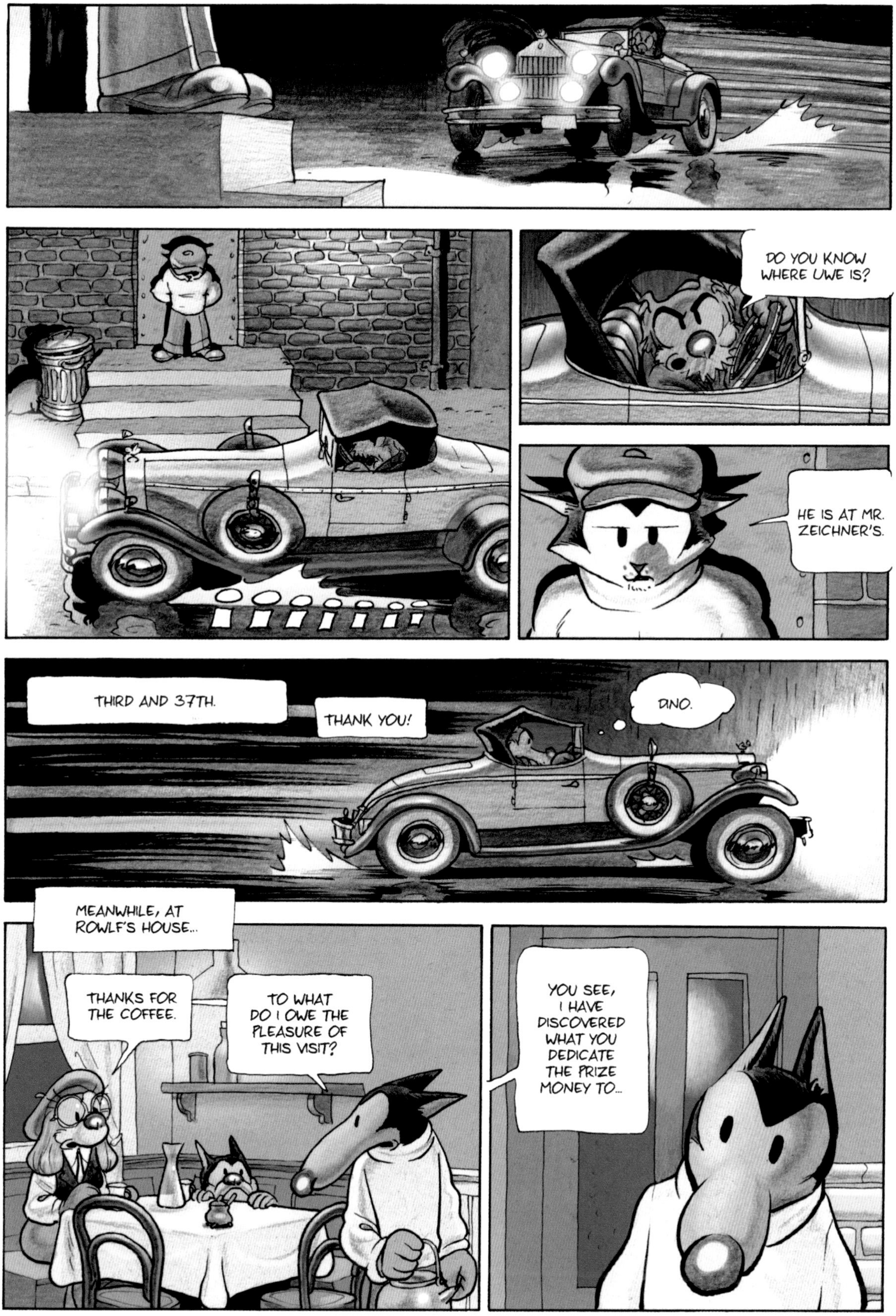
DO YOU KNOW WHERE UWE IS?
HE IS AT MR. ZEICHNER'S.
THIRD AND 37TH.
THANK YOU!
DINO.
MEANWHILE, AT ROWLF'S HOUSE...
THANKS FOR THE COFFEE.
TO WHAT DO I OWE THE PLEASURE OF THIS VISIT?
YOU SEE, I HAVE DISCOVERED WHAT YOU DEDICATE THE PRIZE MONEY TO...

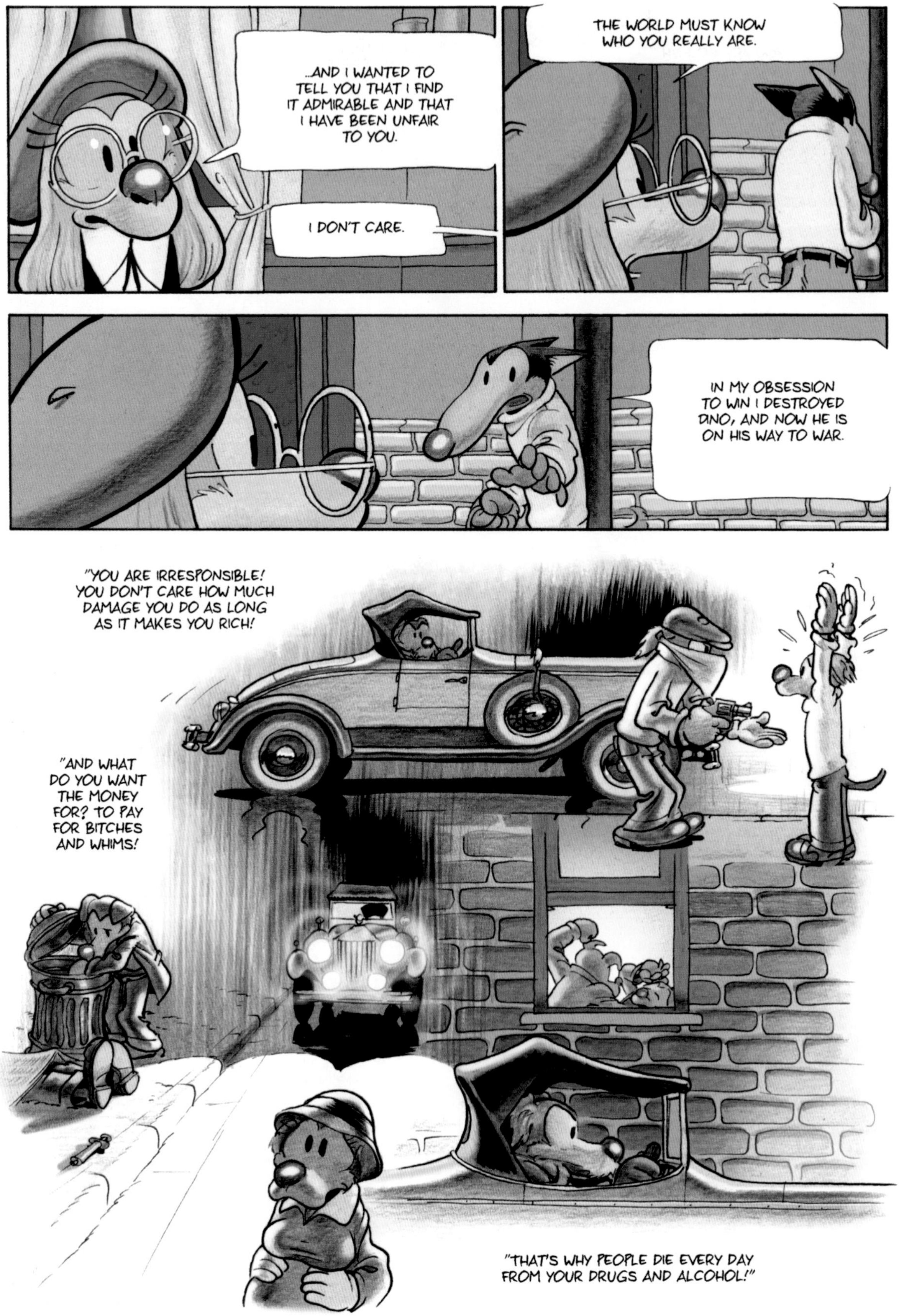
..AND I WANTED TO TELL YOU THAT I FIND IT ADMIRABLE AND THAT I HAVE BEEN UNFAIR TO YOU.
I DON'T CARE.
THE WORLD MUST KNOW WHO YOU REALLY ARE.
IN MY OBSESSION TO WIN I DESTROYED DINO, AND NOW HE IS ON HIS WAY TO WAR.
"YOU ARE IRRESPONSIBLE! YOU DON'T CARE HOW MUCH DAMAGE YOU DO AS LONG AS IT MAKES YOU RICH!
"AND WHAT DO YOU WANT THE MONEY FOR? TO PAY FOR BITCHES AND WHIMS!
"THAT'S WHY PEOPLE DIE EVERY DAY FROM YOUR DRUGS AND ALCOHOL!"

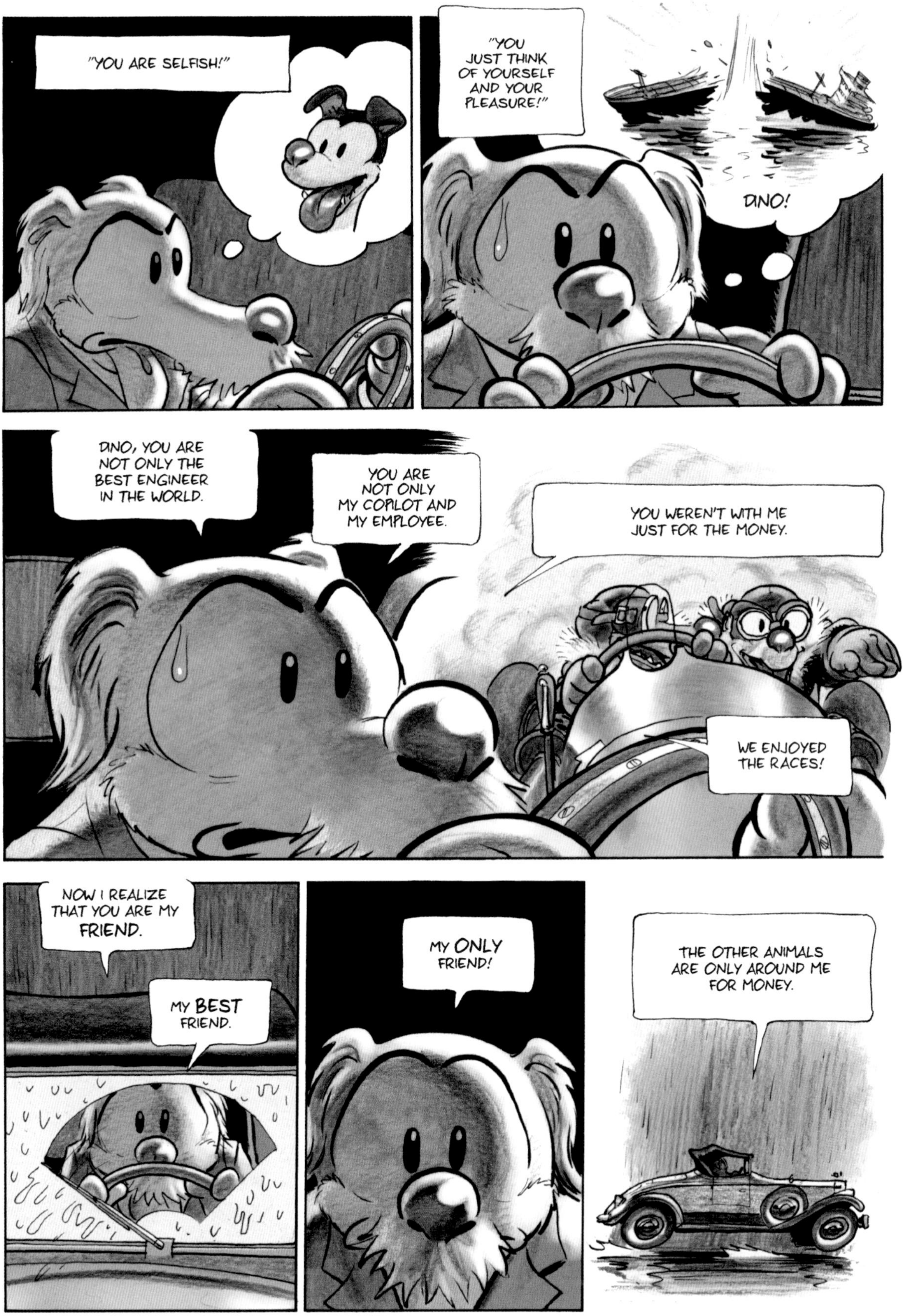

"YOU ARE SELFISH!"
"YOU JUST THINK OF YOURSELF AND YOUR PLEASURE!"
DINO!
DINO, YOU ARE NOT ONLY THE BEST ENGINEER IN THE WORLD.
YOU ARE NOT ONLY MY COPILOT AND MY EMPLOYEE.
YOU WEREN'T WITH ME JUST FOR THE MONEY.
WE ENJOYED THE RACES!
NOW I REALIZE THAT YOU ARE MY FRIEND.
MY BEST FRIEND.
MY ONLY FRIEND!
THE OTHER ANIMALS ARE ONLY AROUND ME FOR MONEY.

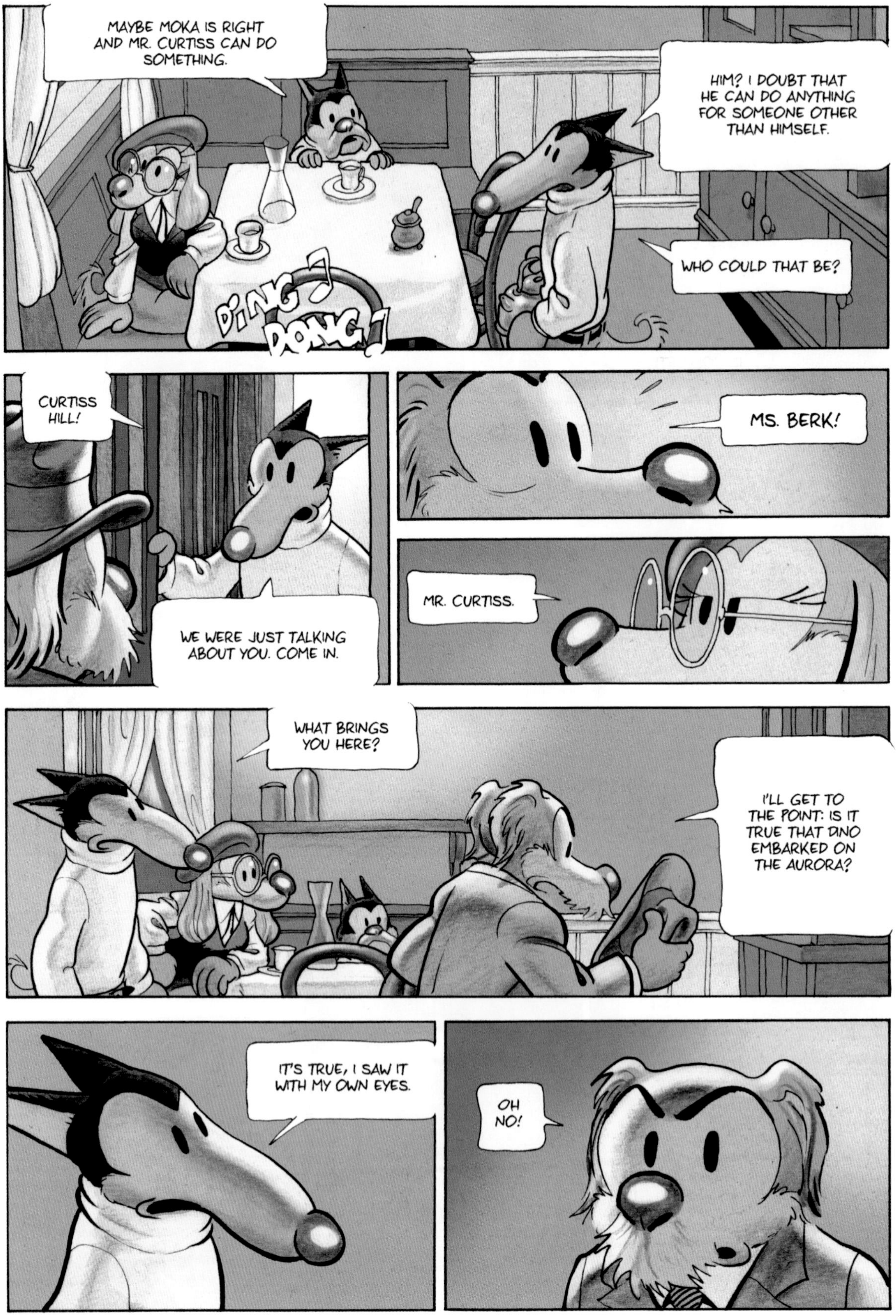

MAYBE MOKA IS RIGHT AND MR. CURTISS CAN DO SOMETHING.
HIM? I DOUBT THAT HE CAN DO ANYTHING FOR SOMEONE OTHER THAN HIMSELF.
DING DONG
WHO COULD THAT BE?
CURTISS HILL!
WE WERE JUST TALKING ABOUT YOU. COME IN.
MS. BERK!
MR. CURTISS.
WHAT BRINGS YOU HERE?
I'LL GET TO THE POINT: IS IT TRUE THAT DINO EMBARKED ON THE AURORA?
IT'S TRUE, I SAW IT WITH MY OWN EYES.
OH NO!

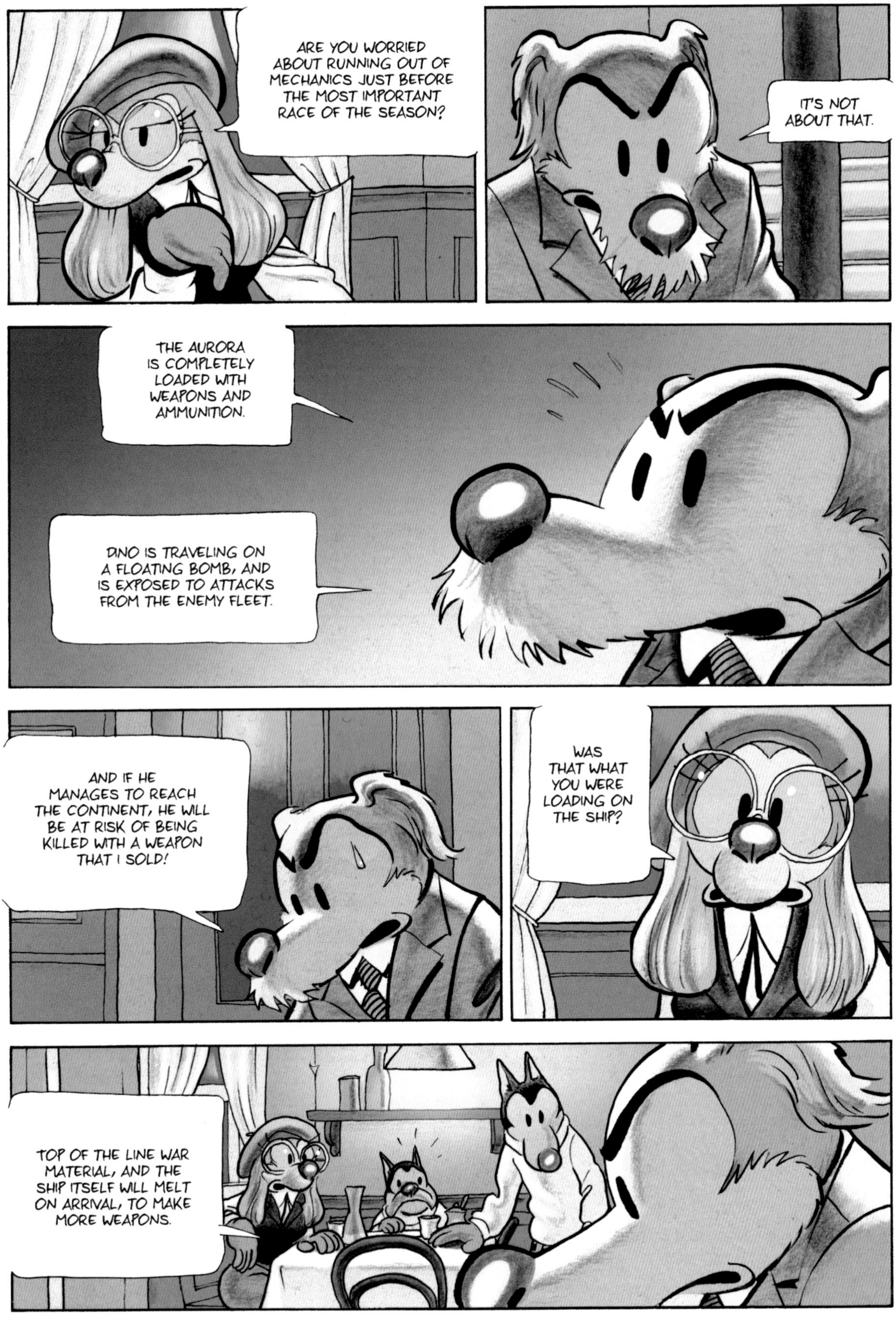
ARE YOU WORRIED ABOUT RUNNING OUT OF MECHANICS JUST BEFORE THE MOST IMPORTANT RACE OF THE SEASON?
IT'S NOT ABOUT THAT.
THE AURORA IS COMPLETELY LOADED WITH WEAPONS AND AMMUNITION.
DINO IS TRAVELING ON A FLOATING BOMB, AND IS EXPOSED TO ATTACKS FROM THE ENEMY FLEET.
AND IF HE MANAGES TO REACH THE CONTINENT, HE WILL BE AT RISK OF BEING KILLED WITH A WEAPON THAT I SOLD!
WAS THAT WHAT YOU WERE LOADING ON THE SHIP?
TOP OF THE LINE WAR MATERIAL, AND THE SHIP ITSELF WILL MELT ON ARRIVAL, TO MAKE MORE WEAPONS.

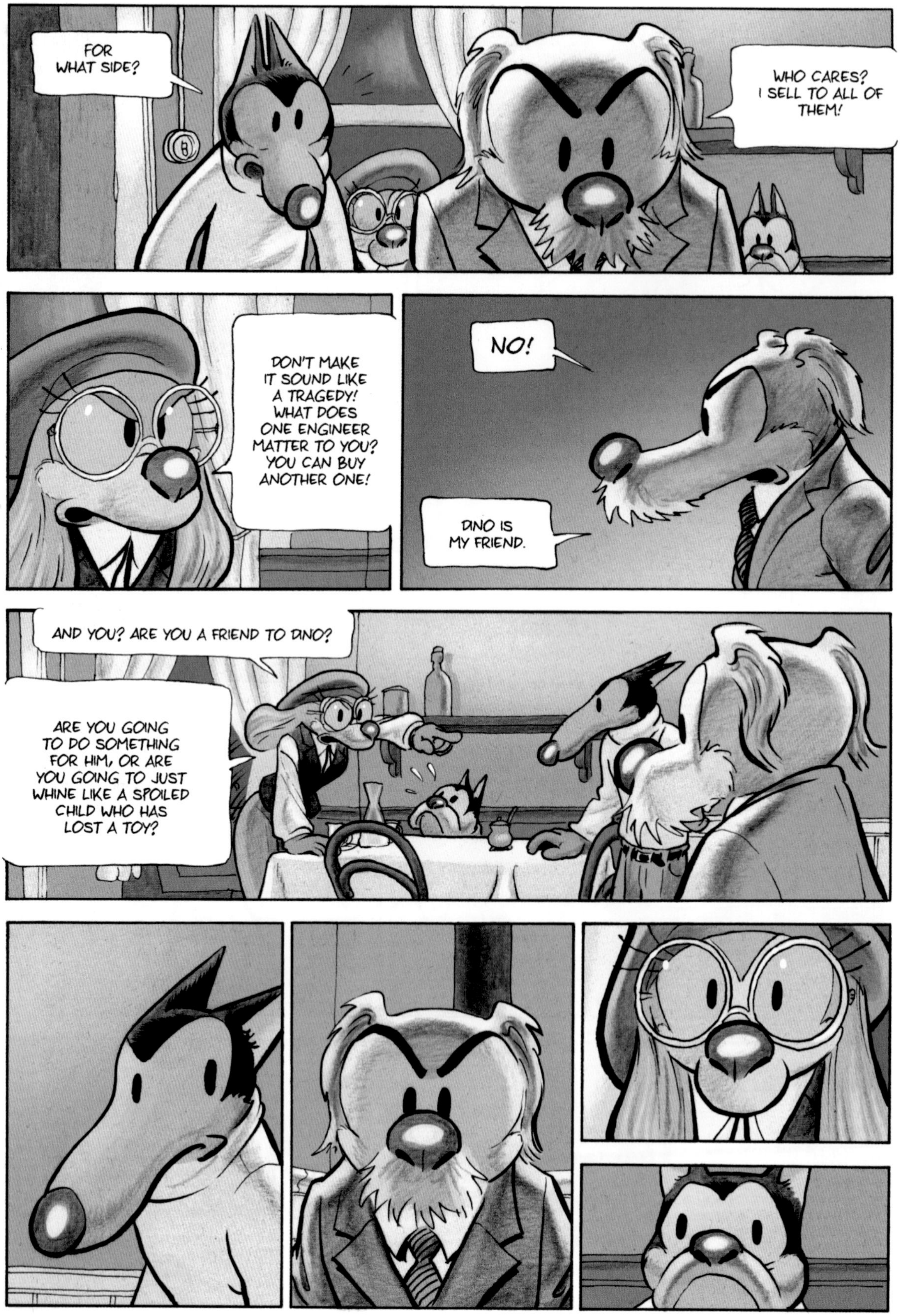
FOR WHAT SIDE?
WHO CARES? I SELL TO ALL OF THEM!
DON'T MAKE IT SOUND LIKE A TRAGEDY! WHAT DOES ONE ENGINEER MATTER TO YOU? YOU CAN BUY ANOTHER ONE!
NO!
DINO IS MY FRIEND.
AND YOU? ARE YOU A FRIEND TO DINO?
ARE YOU GOING TO DO SOMETHING FOR HIM, OR ARE YOU GOING TO JUST WHINE LIKE A SPOILED CHILD WHO HAS LOST A TOY?

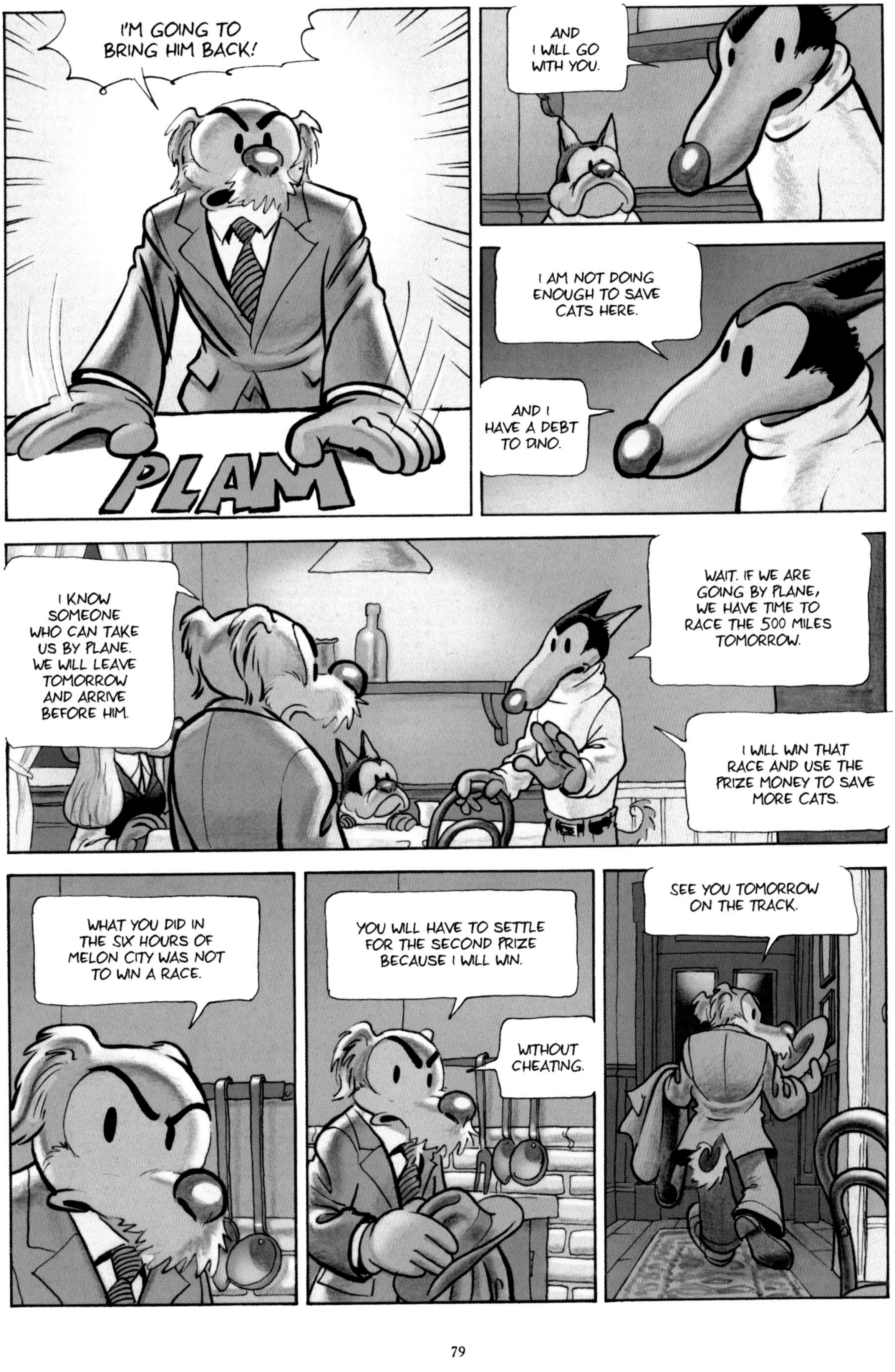
I'M GOING TO BRING HIM BACK!
PLAM
AND I WILL GO WITH YOU.
I AM NOT DOING ENOUGH TO SAVE CATS HERE.
AND I HAVE A DEBT TO DINO.
I KNOW SOMEONE WHO CAN TAKE US BY PLANE. WE WILL LEAVE TOMORROW AND ARRIVE BEFORE HIM.
WAIT. IF WE ARE GOING BY PLANE, WE HAVE TIME TO RACE THE 500 MILES TOMORROW.
I WILL WIN THAT RACE AND USE THE PRIZE MONEY TO SAVE MORE CATS.
WHAT YOU DID IN THE SIX HOURS OF MELON CITY WAS NOT TO WIN A RACE.
YOU WILL HAVE TO SETTLE FOR THE SECOND PRIZE BECAUSE I WILL WIN.
WITHOUT CHEATING.
SEE YOU TOMORROW ON THE TRACK.

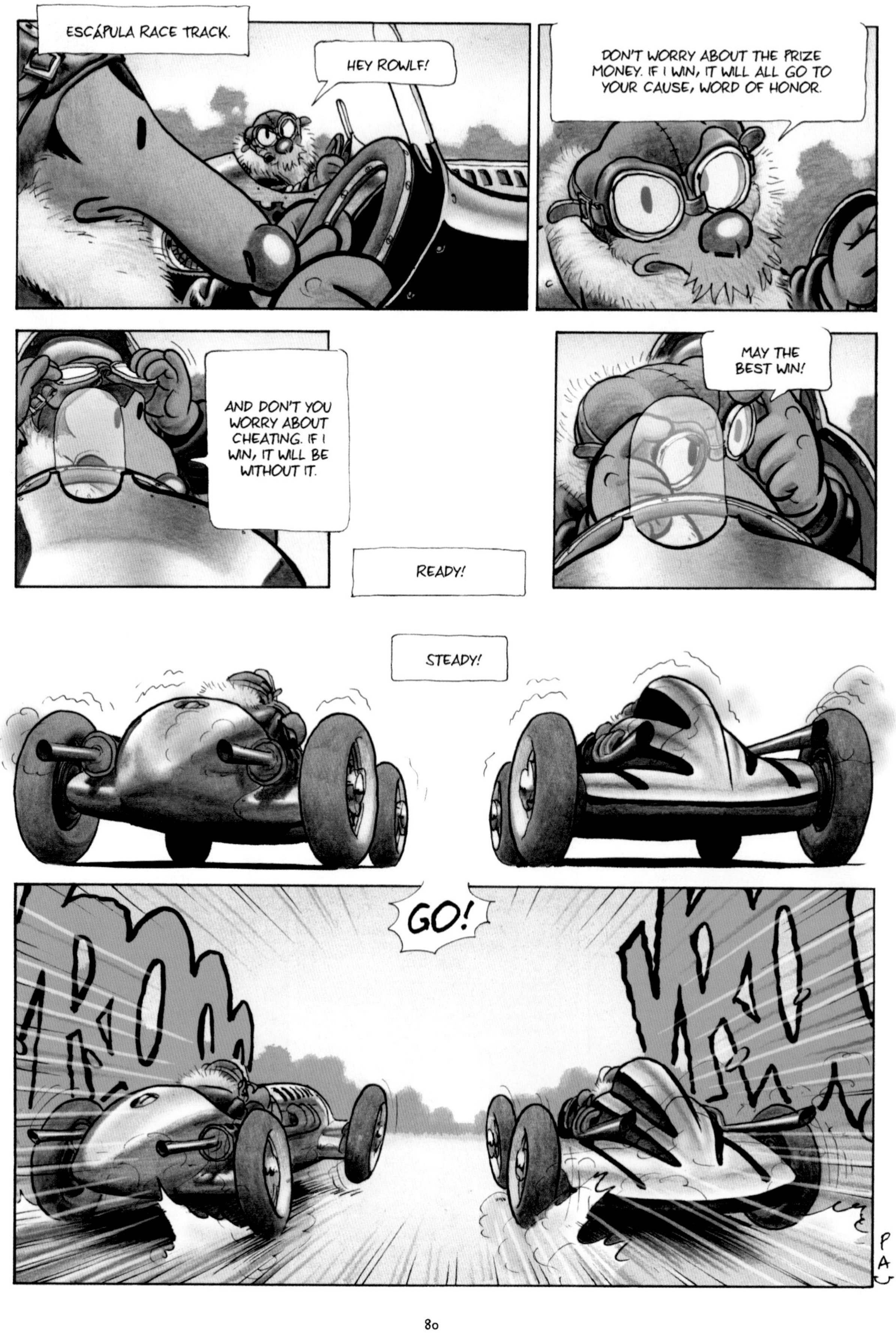

ESCÁPULA RACE TRACK.
HEY ROWLF!
DON'T WORRY ABOUT THE PRIZE MONEY. IF I WIN, IT WILL ALL GO TO YOUR CAUSE, WORD OF HONOR.
AND DON'T YOU WORRY ABOUT CHEATING. IF I WIN, IT WILL BE WITHOUT IT.
MAY THE BEST WIN!
READY!
STEADY!
GO!

Special thanks to my dear patrons, the most loyal readers that gave me the chance to continue dedicating myself to my favorite profession with their generous support:

Åke Mora, Felipe Sánchez-Cuenca, David Vergara Munuera, Empar Rosselló Mora, Samuel Ellington, Guillem Bosch Roca, Shield Bonnichsen, Cristóbal Mora, Michael Foertsch, Francisca Garau, Fernando Sánchez-Cuenca, Daniel Martín Peixe, Raquel Socías, Óscar & Zhuldyz, Nadal Galiana, David & Mauge, LCDR Fish, Germán Socías, Vicente Rodríguez Jiménez-Bravo, Mateo Vallori Nemeckova, Dapzcomic, Sebastià Reus Bustos, Viktor Kalvachev, Bernardo & Silvia, Jonathan D. Phillips, Jordan Mello, José Carlos Cerro Garrido, Iván García, Júnior, Óscar Luis Pérez, Ricard valdivielso, Joaquín Rodríguez Jiménez-Bravo, José Antonio García Perelló, Mike Doggo, Nomisx, James Lloyd, Paco Asenjo, Timothy Llompart, Olga Serrano, Erik Jay Weber, Aina, Dina, Leo VF, Gonzalo Aeneas, Alex Fito, Alexis Fajardo, Toni Nicolau, Ángel Prieto, Daniel Acuña, Alex Otaku, El Gamer, Matíes Barceló, A. Fraser, Alejandro Maestro, and Javi Godoy.

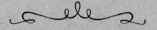

Join us at **www.patreon.com/pau** !

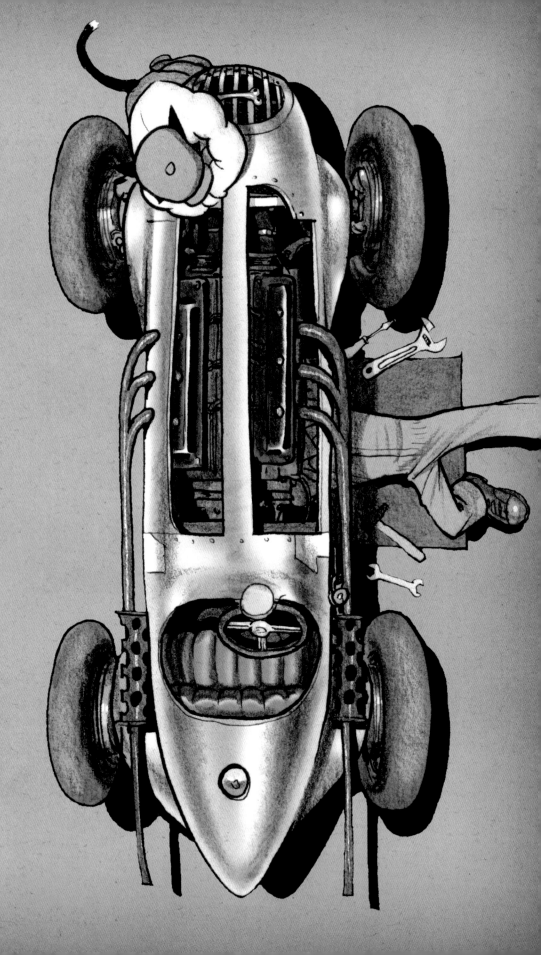

Curtiss Hill

original sketches by
PAU

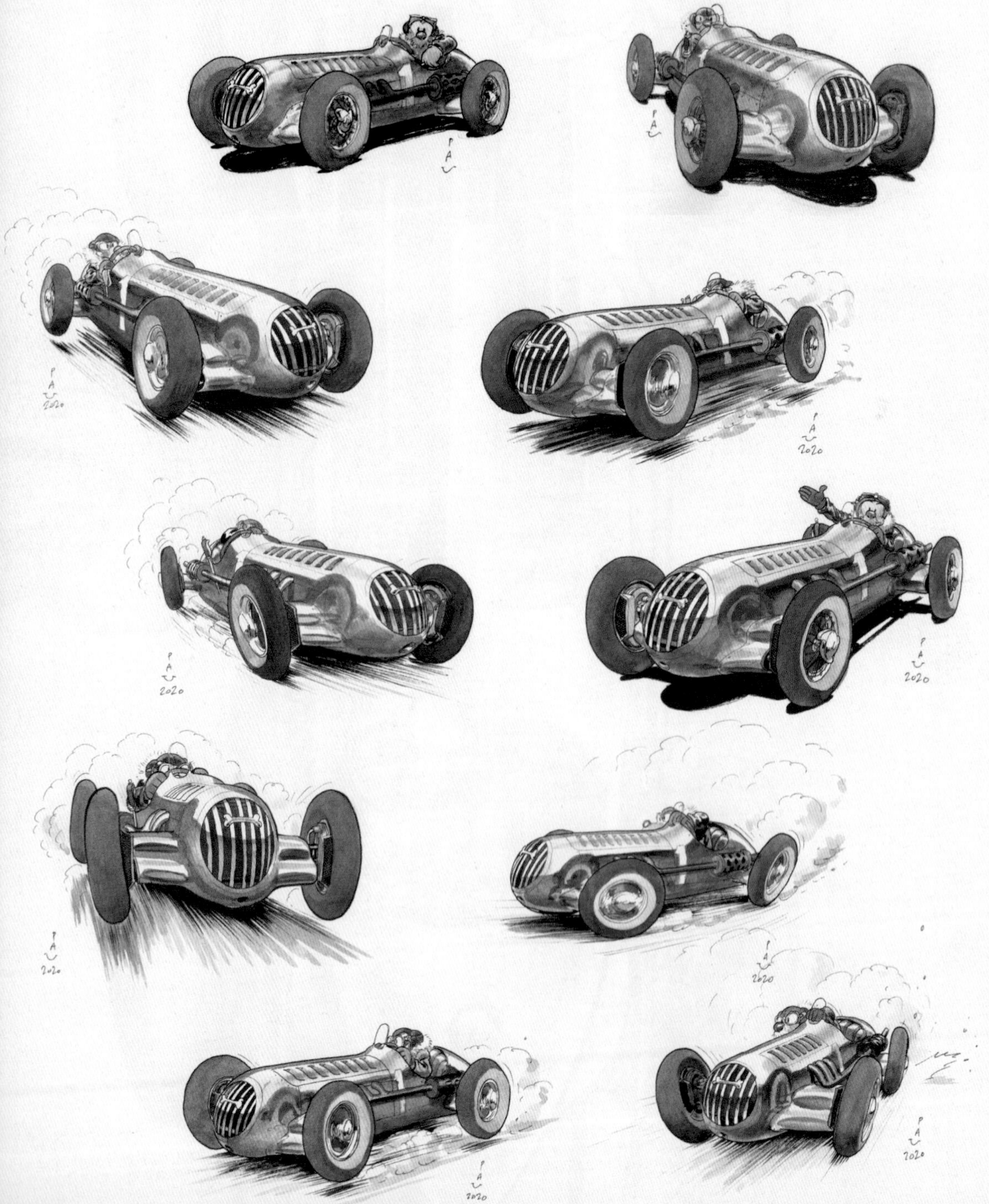

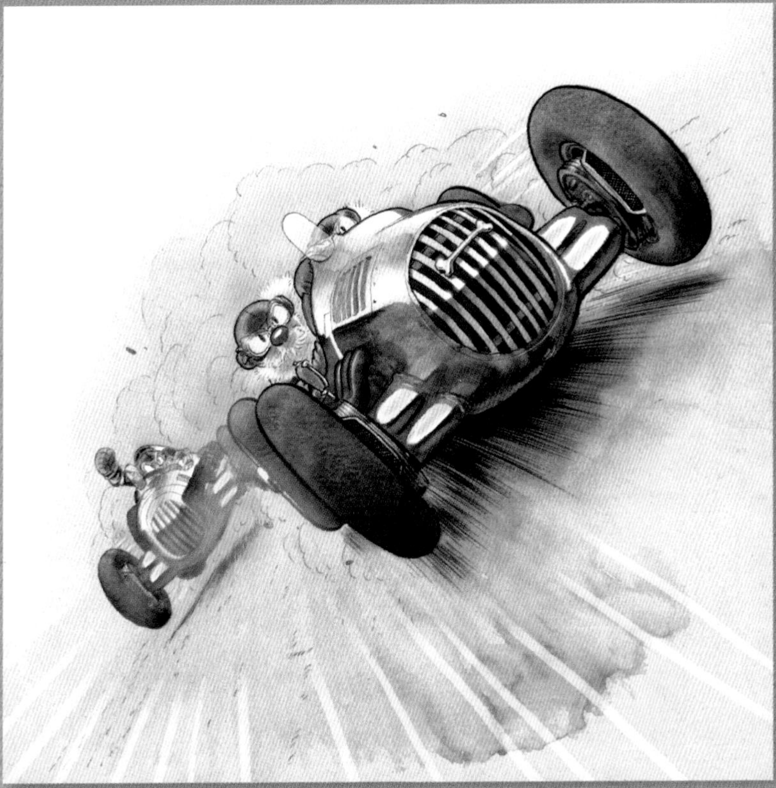

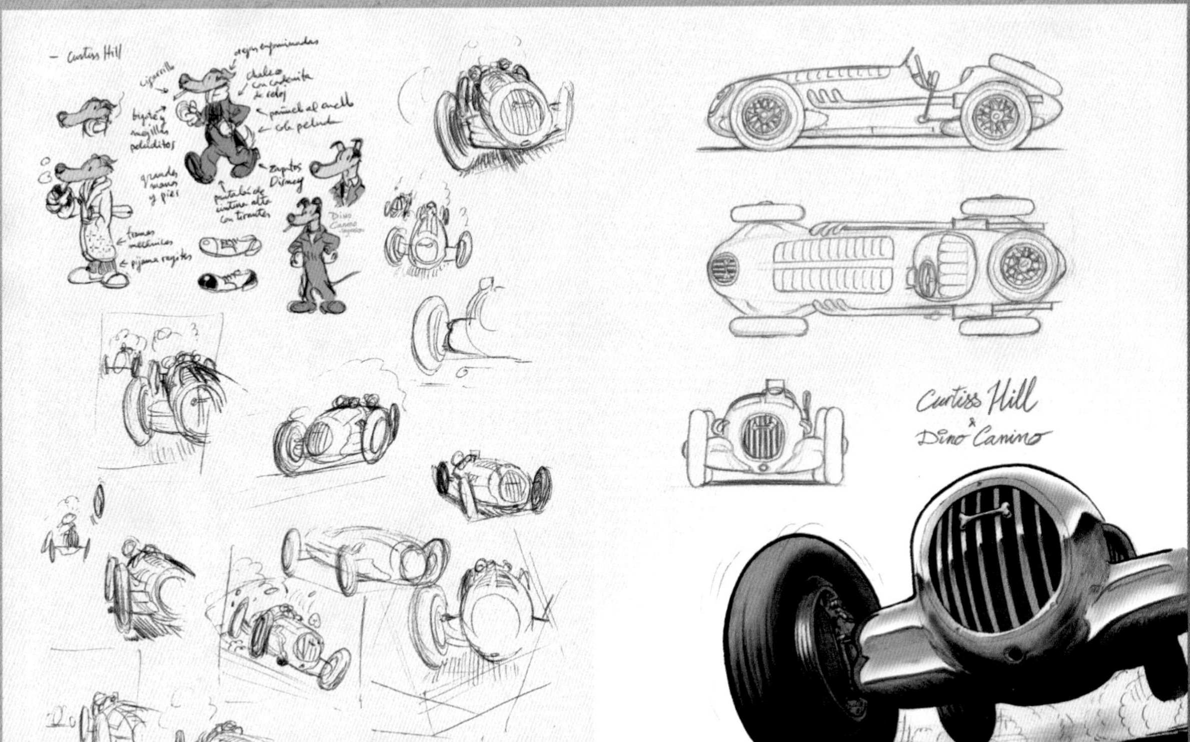
- Curtiss Hill
grandes manos y pies
Zapatos Disney
Curtiss Hill & Dino Canino

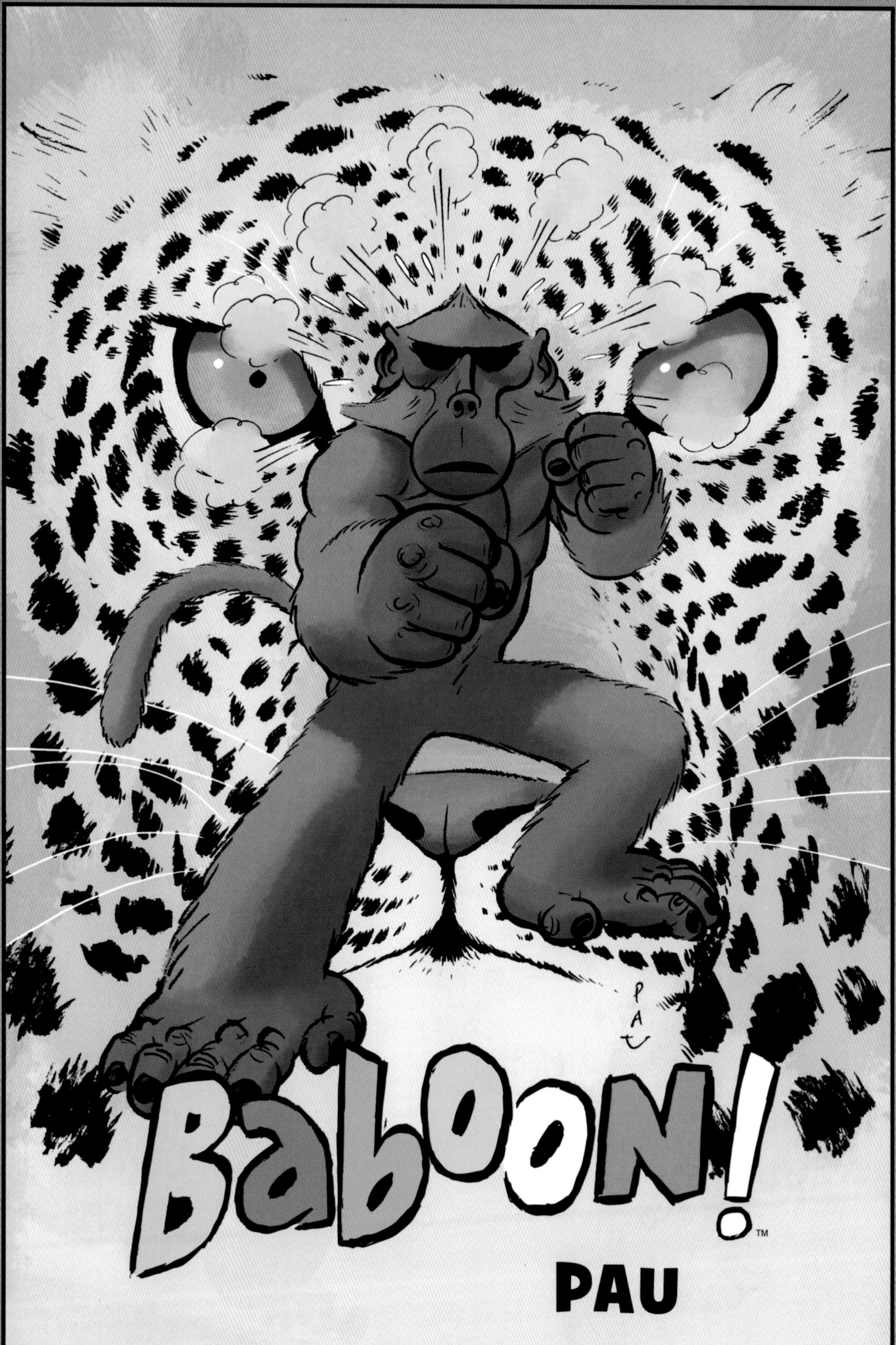
BABOON!™
PAU

ALSO AVAILABLE FROM DARK HORSE BOOKS!

BABOON!

A BABOON FIGHTS ITS WAY BACK TO ITS RIGHTFUL SPOT IN THE ANIMAL KINGDOM IN THIS WONDERFULLY ILLUSTRATED, WORDLESS GRAPHIC NOVEL BY REVERED SPANISH WRITER AND ARTIST PAU, AUTHOR OF *ATLAS & AXIS*!

After the death of its adopted leopard mother, an orphaned baboon wanders the wild in search of companionship and a sense of identity. Stumbling upon the troop of baboons from which it was originally stolen, the baboon falls in love with the troop's head female. Initially rejected, beaten, and discarded by the alpha baboon of the troop, the orphaned baboon trains to fight and earn its respect in the animal kingdom!

DARK HORSE BOOKS

ISBN 978-1-50671-795-1 • $14.99 US | $19.99 CAN